THE LITT

Chocolate

Katherine Khodorowsky
Hervé Robert

Flammarion

Now an everyday item, chocolate no longer exudes a certain aura of exoticism as it once did. But where does it come from? How is its consumption divided from continent to continent, and in what forms?

The cacao tree, like the coffee bush, thrives in tropical climes. Its seed—the bean—undergoes numerous different processes before it reaches the consumer. How does cocoa become chocolate?

Dark or milk, flavored or filled, chocolate offers a tremendous range of tastes to the connoisseur. How are new recipes created, and by whom? Do different countries have different national preferences?

A N S W E R S

Orientation p. 6

The book presents the world of chocolate, drawing together the articles which appear in the Alphabetical Guide according to three different perspectives, each with its own colour code.

■ The product:
forms,
recipes,
countries.

■ The process:
cultivation,
manufacture,
enjoyment.

■ The context:
history,
pioneers,
economic background.

By following these articles, with their cross-references indicated by asterisks, the reader will be able to explore the book—and the world of chocolate—at leisure.

The Story of Chocolate p. 11

The book opens with a brief survey of the A *to* Z section, setting out its structure and developing its main themes and topics.

Alphabetical Guide p. 29

Arranged in alphabetical order, the articles in this section contain all you need to know about chocolate. The information they contain is complemented by the following;
- detailed notes on the principal manufacturing nations and the major consumers of chocolate
- highlighted panels exploring key topics.

ORIENTATION

I. FROM LEGEND TO HISTORY

A. The "brown gold" of the New World

In the early sixteenth century, the conquistadors set out to find the land of Eldorado; instead they discovered a "brown gold," used to make a creamy but pungent drink. Soon the chocolate of the Aztecs, sweetened with cane sugar and retaining all its evident invigorating properties, was to conquer the Spaniards.

- *Aphrodisiac*
- *Aztecs*
- *Church*
- *Cortés (Hernán)*
- *Cult*
- *Etymology*
- *Quetzalcoatl*
- *Spain*
- **Spice**

B. The conquest of Europe

Within two centuries, chocolate's conquest of Europe was complete. From 1580, Spanish ships were unloading cargoes of cocoa beans in their native ports. Anne of Austria introduced chocolate at the French court. Scholars, travellers and merchants brought it to Italy and across the Alps. A French *chocolatier* took it to London.

- **Austria and Germany**
- *Bayonne*
- **Belgium**
- *Chocolate houses*
- **France**
- **Great Britain**
- **Italy**
- **Netherlands**
- **Switzerland**
- *Versailles*

C. The modern revolution

For many years in Continental Europe, chocolate—as a drink or in pastille form—remained a luxury commodity, reserved for the aristocracy. The industrial revolution, the spirit of enterprise and the genius of certain inventors were to combine to make chocolate available to the middle classes. Now the first industrial chocolate factories were able to produce chocolate in large quantities and at a lower price.

- *Caffarel*
- *Hershey (Milton)*
- *Menier (Émile-Justin)*
- *Neuhaus (Jean)*
- *Poulain (Victor-Auguste)*
- *Suchard (Philippe)*

II. CHOCOLATE IN ALL ITS FORMS

A. A jewel of nature

The cacao tree is cultivated in tropical countries, and the beans are generally treated in the place of cultivation. The most complex processes in their transformation take place in Europe and the United States, where the beans are industrially turned into cocoa paste and then into chocolate.

- ■ *Beans*
- ■ *Cacao tree*
- ■ *Cocoa butter*
- ■ *Confectioners' coating*
- ■ *Cultivation*
- ■ *Manufacturing process*
- ■ *Paste*
- ■ *Powder*
- ■ *Varieties*

B. The metamorphoses of chocolate

Poured into molds in liquid form, chocolate emerges in the shape of bars, Easter eggs and cases for filling. In *pâtisserie*, it is used as the main ingredient and as icing. Now an everyday product in many different guises, it also ranks as a gourmet item, thanks to the skills of master *chocolatiers*.

- ■ *Banania*
- ■ *Bars*
- ■ *Chocolates*
- ■ *Confectionery*
- ■ *Easter*
- ■ *Hot chocolate*
- ■ *Ices*
- ■ *Molding*
- ■ *Pâtisserie*
- ■ *Truffle*

C. A stake in the market

The third largest commodity on the world market, after sugar and coffee, cocoa is quoted on the stock markets of London, New York and Paris. The financial stakes are high, and it remains a vital factor in the economies of producer nations. In Europe, the manufacturing process is divided between major industrial concerns and small craft industries, each helping to ensure both quality and variety.

- ■ *Factories*
- ■ *Market*
- ■ *Master chocolatier*
- ■ *Plantation*
- ■ *Producer nations*
- ■ *Regulation*
- ■ *Tax*

III. A WORLD OF PLEASURES

A. The alchemy of tastes

Dark, milk or white; filled with cream, praline, ganache or liqueur; savoured with coffee or a fruit brandy: chocolate offers a tremendous variety of flavours and taste associations, constantly broadened in scope by creative talents.

- ■ *Alcoholic drinks*
- ■ *Coffee*
- ■ *Dark chocolate*
- ■ *Fruit and nuts*
- ■ *Ganache*
- ■ *Liqueur chocolates*
- ■ *Milk chocolate*
- ■ *Praline*
- ■ *White chocolate*

B. Chocolate euphoria

Valued for centuries as a fortifying tonic, chocolate is now recognized by dietitians as being of nutritional value, and has shaken off its doubtful reputation. In moderate quantities, it may be consumed without fear its stimulating and mood-enhancing properties—or for the sake of sheer pleasure.

- ▨ *Consumption*
- ■ *Drug*
- ■ *Health*
- ▨ *Iron rations*
- ■ *Nutritional qualities*
- ■ *Storage*
- ▨ *Treatise* ✎

C. A source of inspiration

Once an exotic pleasure, now a symbol of gourmet indulgence, chocolate has found a place in literature and art: sumptuous services in porcelain or silver, *trembleuse* cups and *chocolatières*, still life paintings and novels all bear witness to its importance in Western culture.

- ▨ *Advertising*
- ▨ *Brillat-Savarin*
- ■ *Chocolate box*
- ■ *Chocolatière*
- ■ *Club*
- ▨ *Collecting*
- ■ *Cup*
- ▨ *Design*
- ▨ *Fashion*
- ▨ *Literature*
- ▨ *Masterpiece*
- ▨ *Painting*

légende
légende

THE STORY OF CHOCOLATE

S ome things never change. Take a group of people in any context—work, leisure, sport, culture. Take from your pocket or
bag a bar of chocolate. At this point, the assembled company will
invariably split into two factions: those who maintain an air of stu-
dious indifference, and those who fall over themselves in their haste
to request a share in your sinful indulgence.

Connoisseurs of dark or bitter chocolate, aficionados of French
ganache or Belgian praline, lovers of Swiss milk chocolate or creamy
white bars, devotees faithful to simple childish treats or epicureans
in search of more sophisticated pleasures—these are only some of
the innumerable fraternity whom chocolate holds in its thrall...

1. From legend to history
A. The "brown gold" of the New World

The etymology* of the word "chocolate" may remain uncertain and
open to debate even today, but there can be no real doubt that the
ancient Aztec* civilization lies at the origin of chocolate. The god
Quetzalcoatl, gardener of paradise, was venerated as guardian of the
cacao tree, purveyor of both strength and wealth. The seeds, or
beans,* were used as a form of currency, valid both
for the purchase of everyday items and for the
payment of tribute money to the king.

It was the spectacle of monkeys and squirrels sucking the refreshing pulp surrounding the beans that first gave men the idea of
tasting it. From there, it was a short step to
consuming the beans themselves. Who was
it who first had the idea of roasting the
beans and crushing them into a paste?
Nobody knows. But in the course of time,
the sophisticated Aztec civilization discovered how to flavor cocoa paste* with spices*
in order to make a nourishing and invigorat-
ing drink, as useful to the poor, as a supplement to their staple diet
of maize broth, as it was pleasurable to the king, Montezuma II, as a
source of gastronomic delight.

When, in 1502, Christopher Columbus was presented with some
cocoa beans by an Indian chief, he failed to realize the value of this
gift, as he had only visited the coastal zone of this land of "New
Spain" and was not yet familiar with its customs. Not until the

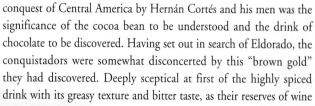

Previous page:
Pre-Columbian
statuette
of Quetzalcoatl.
Musée
de l'Homme,
Paris.

conquest of Central America by Hernán Cortés and his men was the significance of the cocoa bean to be understood and the drink of chocolate to be discovered. Having set out in search of Eldorado, the conquistadors were somewhat disconcerted by this "brown gold" they had discovered. Deeply sceptical at first of the highly spiced drink with its greasy texture and bitter taste, as their reserves of wine ran out they found themselves becoming accustomed to it. Sweetened with cane sugar, and fortified by its restorative properties and its reputation as an aphrodisiac, the chocolate drink invaded their daily lives. And with it came a better understanding of the importance of the cacao tree and of the symbolic significance of the cults that surrounded it.

The Spanish rapidly became passionate devotees of the new beverage, which promptly gave rise to interminable disputes between different factions within the church* on the vexed question of whether or not liquid chocolate broke the fast: the beverage had become particularly popular in ecclesiastical circles, notably on days when the eating of meat was forbidden.

Above:
*Portrait
of the Emperor
Montezuma,*
eighteenth
century.

B. The conquest of Europe

Cortés had brought the first cocoa beans back to Charles V in 1528. Yet it was not until 1580 that the conquistadors, who up to that point had zealously hoarded this treasure for themselves, were obliged to resign themselves to sending cargoes of beans to Spain. Chocolate now began to be manufactured on the Iberian peninsula, and before long, commercial exchanges, the curiosity of travelers, and royal marriages had combined to ensure the spread of hot chocolate, the drink of aristocrats, throughout Europe.

The trading ports of Flanders and the Low Countries (then a possession of Philip II of Spain) discovered the beverage in the late sixteenth century, though they remained in ignorance of the recipe, which was jealously guarded by the Spanish. Only in 1606 was it brought out of Spain, by the Florentine merchant Antonio Carletti, whereupon it was swiftly adopted as a restorative by Italian doctors.

The arrival of chocolate in France* was for many years attributed (though doubtfully, it now appears) to Jewish chocolate-makers who,

hounded out of Spain and then Portugal, settled in Bayonne,* near the Spanish border, from 1609. It owed its official introduction to Anne of Austria, daughter of Philip III of Spain, who married Louis XIII in 1615. The vogue for chocolate continued at Versailles* under Louis XIV and gained in strength under Louis XV. The first French *chocolatier*, David Chaillou, acquired a twenty-nine-year monopoly on the sale and production of chocolate "as liquor or pastilles," and in 1671 opened the first premises in Paris selling "drinking chocolate."

A scholar who arrived from Italy across the Alps in 1640 was the first to bring chocolate into Austria,* where monasteries were responsible for its spread throughout the country. The following year, another scholar returning from Naples to his native Germany* brought with him the precious recipe.

In 1657, chocolate arrived in Great Britain,* where the fashion for drinking it soon began to rival the vogue for coffee. Eating chocolate, sold in the form of "Spanish rolls," also became a popular delicacy

Jean-Étienne
Liotard,
*Le Petit
Déjeuner*,
1753–6.
Pastel
on parchment.
Alte Pinakothek,
Munich.

Lindt-Sprüngli factory, Kilchberg, c.1899.

from 1674. In 1697, London saw the opening of the first chocolate houses,* convivial establishments for gaming, discussing politics and drinking the fashionable beverage.

Switzerland* came late to chocolate: it was introduced there by Italian merchants in 1750. But another 150 years were to pass and many new techniques and inventions to be perfected before chocolate was to accomplish its universal and popular conquest of Europe.

C. The modern revolution

Established originally by apothecaries in the eighteenth century to make medicinal chocolates, chocolate factories* were to remain small-scale, unmechanized cottage industries for two centuries. Early nineteenth-century advances in the harnessing of hydraulic energy and the use of steam-driven machinery opened the way for the production of chocolate in large quantities and at low cost, and encouraged the development of specialist industries.

A fall in the price of sugar, the reduction in manufacturing costs and the general rise in living standards across Europe together

combined to ensure the democratization of chocolate. By the early twentieth century, chocolate had become an integral part of almost every child's breakfast and tea-time treats. In France, Menier* and Poulain* were the pioneers of this growing industry, destined to make chocolate available to all. Refusing to compromise on quality, Émile-Justin Menier appropriated the means of control of the entire production process, from cultivation* on the plantations* to distribution in the shops. A progressive employer, he took care to ensure the wellbeing of his employees and also followed a political career. Victor-Auguste Poulain, meanwhile, was determined to reconcile low prices and high quality, and in this constant quest put himself in the forefront of technical developments and in the use of advertising.*

Elsewhere in Europe, other inventive spirits were busily engaged in revolutionizing the chocolate industry. In the Netherlands, Coenraad Van Houten developed a process for making cocoa powder* by extracting the cocoa butter,* complementing his invention by perfecting a technique to ensure greater solubility. In Switzerland* in 1875, Daniel Peter became the first to produce milk chocolate. In

Advertisement for Suchard cocoa powder, c.1890.

15

Previous pages:
Freshly
picked pods,
Cameroon.

Cocoa beans.

Italy,* Caffarel* (Paolo Caffarelli) created the recipe for the hazelnut and almond chocolate that came to be known as *gianduja*. In Belgium,* Jean Neuhaus invented first the praline chocolate and then the cardboard *ballotin*, now the traditional packaging for numerous chocolate assortments. And finally, again in Switzerland, Philippe Suchard* earned worldwide fame largely through the success of his celebrated milk chocolate bar, Milka.

II. Chocolate in all its forms
A. A jewel of nature

No, chocolate bars do not grow on cacao trees! The fruit (or pod) of the cacao tree and the seeds (or beans) it contains undergo a lengthy and complex series of transformations in order to yield their end product—in this case, chocolate.

It all starts with the selection of the botanical varieties for cultivation: as with vines, each has its own specific personality. After harvesting, the pulp and seeds are removed from the pods, and the beans undergo two processes of fermentation. Dried, sorted and checked, they are then generally exported for processing.

Roasting
workshop.

In the factories,* the beans are shelled and roasted to develop their aromas, before being crushed, ground and refined to produce a cocoa

paste.* At this point, the making of chocolate as we know it begins, with the blending of pastes derived from different varieties, selected according to the desired final flavour, and the addition of sugar, vanilla and sometimes milk powder. The ingredients are carefully mixed and passed through a rolling mill, before being conched and tempered. At the end of all this, the chocolate may be poured into molds to make bars.* Alternatively, the cocoa paste may be pressed in order to extract the cocoa butter;* the dry residue, known as "cake," is then used as the basis of cocoa powder.*

The ingenuity of the first tribes who took this unpromising-looking fruit and seed and transformed them into a delectable indulgence can only be admired!

B. The metamorphoses of chocolate

No other food product can rival chocolate's magical ability to assume so many different forms.

Poured into molds in liquid form, it may reappear in the shape of bars, Easter* eggs, individual shells to be filled, or confectionery* products. Or instead it may become the finest of powders, rich dark brown in colour, to be combined effortlessly with milk to make warming, invigorating hot chocolate.* With the addition of flour, it

"Frame molding," used to make individual chocolates.

becomes a satisfying breakfast drink. Or it may transform itself into a dazzling array of individual chocolates, concealing within their fine chocolate coating a mouthwatering assortment of fillings. Refreshing in ice* creams and sorbets, it is also one of the noblest ingredients in *pâtisserie.** The tremendous diversity of chocolate and the continuing improvement in the quality of the mass-produced product together ensure constant growth in an already immense market. Not only is it a product for everyday consumption, at any hour of the day; it has also taken its place, in the last decade or so, in the rarefied company of foodstuffs which may be considered to be truly gastronomic products. No gourmet restaurant menu is complete without a dessert based on bitter chocolate, and coffee* is more often than not served accompanied by wafer-thin *napolitains* or dainty individual choco-

Drying cocoa beans, Cameroon, *c.*1930.

lates. Finally, of course, comes the sublime, darkly sophisticated truffle,* a ball of ganache* rolled in cocoa powder to resemble its namesake, that other symbol of French gastronomy.

C. A stake in the market

In the wake of chocolate's success in Europe, cultivation of the cacao tree spread across the globe. For economic reasons, Britain, France, the Low Countries and Portugal had already founded colonies in countries enjoying climates propitious to the cultivation of spices, and now they established cacao plantations in these same fertile lands. As demand in Europe grew, the cacao tree spread from Central America to the West Indies, South America and finally Africa. The third largest commodity on the world market* after sugar and coffee, cocoa was for many years subject to sudden, repeated and extreme fluctuations in price, a reflection of tensions between the producer and processing nations. As a result, industrial manufacturers of coating chocolate (see Confectioners' coating) in the principal consumer countries have set up processing plants to produce semi-finished cocoa products (cocoa butter, cake, powder) in the producer nations.* Relations remain tense, however, and the cocoa prices fixed in the markets of London, New York and Paris are occasionally subject to speculation by powerful bidders, who thus have great power over the producer countries. The composition of different kinds of chocolate is required to conform to strict regulations,* introduced to combat the sale of adulterated products. All countries in Europe have now received authorization to replace 5 percent of the cocoa butter with vegetable fats. Although this move reduces the cost of production, not all the major manufacturers are in favor of it, believing that chocolate is thereby debased and the doors opened to other possible abuses. Moreover, it has dramatic consequences for the economies of producer nations, most of which are part of the developing world. The Ivory Coast, the world's leading producer, has nevertheless tried to deal with the problem by encouraging the cultivation of the shea tree for the production of an alternative to cocoa butter to be used in chocolate.

Drying cocoa beans, Ivory Coast.

III. A world of pleasures
A. The alchemy of tastes

Chameleon-like, chocolate may change its color according to the whim of its makers. The color and flavor of dark chocolate* vary according to the beans that go into its composition. Confusing a high cocoa content and exaggerated bitterness with quality, consumers have sometimes tended to push this to extremes. Milk chocolate* is still the most popular with consumers, with recipes adapted to different national tastes. Switzerland remains faithful to the taste for chocolate with a high milk content. In Belgium, chocolate is

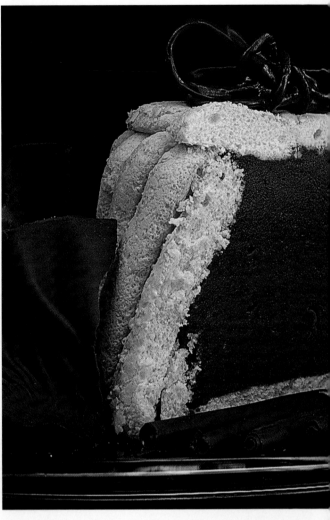

richer in cream and melts more easily. The confectionery-loving British and Americans like it with a slight taste of toffee. The French prefer it with less sugar and fat in order to let the taste of good-quality beans come through. And as for white chocolate,* although it has no rightful claim to call itself chocolate at all, it makes an attractive decoration for chocolate and molded figures.

The language of chocolate, like that of wine, is rich in sensual connotations, and it also lends itself to the evocation of gastronomic alliances designed to intensify the pleasure on the palate. Partnered by a liqueur or spirit to complement its aroma, or by a dose of hot, strong coffee, chocolate creates a kaleidoscope of intoxicating and wickedly "addictive" sensations on the tongue.

The fillings inside the fine, protective casings of individual chocolates are designed to melt quickly in the mouth, leaving a lingering

Chocolate
charlotte.

taste of their delectable aroma. They fall into three main categories—
a cream or butter-based mixture, praline* or ganache*—within
which they may assume an infinite variety of forms, according to the
flair and imagination of the master *chocolatier* who creates them. The
first is usually made with fondant sugar and used to fill the molded
shells of Belgian praline chocolates (not to be confused with praline
itself), the semi-liquid filling contrasting with the solid casing. In
praline, hazelnuts and almonds mingle their aromas and oils and are
suspended in sheets of toffee, which are then crushed with metic-
ulous care. Meanwhile, ganache, an epicurean confection of cocoa,
cream and sometimes butter, offers a voluptuous harmony of bitter
and sweet, tart and creamy. It may be flavoured with spices, alcoholic
essences or candied fruit* in a virtuoso exercise in the delicate association of flavors, a testament to the finesse of the *chocolatier's* art.

Previous page:
Chocolate by
Barry Callebaut.

B. Chocolate euphoria

The most prolific consumers of chocolate have always
been the western European countries and the United
States; this pattern may change in the future, however,
with the growth of the Brazilian, Chinese and Japanese markets. The inhabitants of producer countries,
which are generally poor and export the crop as a
source of foreign revenue, eat little chocolate. In any
case, chocolate requires a dry, temperate climate for
optimal storage* conditions.

Although chocolate is now viewed as an indulgence
(and a deliciously sinful one at that), for many years
it was appreciated chiefly for its invigorating and fortifying properties, particularly by the military. The
formidable warriors of the Aztec armies drew strength
from it; Napoleon I is said to have drunk quantities
of it on the battlefield; and more recently, it was
included in the rations of American G.I.s.

For centuries, chocolate was also considered as a
remedy for various ills, as is clear from numerous
learned treatises written by travellers returning from
the New World and by members of the medical pro-
fession. Nowadays, concerned as we are with our
health* and with enjoying a balanced diet, we are
interested above all in its nutritional qualities.* Nutritionists have
now exonerated chocolate from the bad press it has received, con-
firming on the contrary not only that it does possess nutritional
properties that are beyond dispute, but also that it has a tonic and
mood-enhancing effect. Scientific research has also refuted a good
deal of other beliefs surrounding this confectionery. Chocolate's
virtues as an aphrodisiac, so ardently claimed for so long, now appear
to lie in the realms of fantasy. Nor can it claim to be addictive. Nevertheless, it will always be assured a place of honor in the pharma-
copoeia of pleasure...

C. A source of inspiration

With its wealth of symbolism, chocolate has proved a source of inspiration for a variety of art forms. Lauded by Anthelme Brillat-Savarin*
and alternately eulogized and lambasted by Madame de Sévigné in her
correspondence, it has appeared in the pages of many novels. The plastic arts have also played their part in its celebration, and the

picturesque paraphernalia of chocolate-making—*trembleuse* cups,* delicately worked *chocolatières* and sumptuous porcelain or silver services—became a feature of many still lifes and other paintings. Chocolate itself has become the medium for sculpted masterpieces* by apprentices or experienced *chocolatiers* in professional competitions. In the world of fashion,* designers have found their inspiration in chocolate: chocolate-coated dresses have even been known to grace the catwalk. The aesthetic concerns that are never far from chocolate also find their expression in advertising,* in packaging and chocolate boxes* and in the creative flair shown in new ranges of chocolates.

Museums, shows and trade fairs have been devoted to chocolate. "Fanatics" gather in clubs* to taste it and collect objects associated with it: vintage advertisements, molds, postage stamps, *chocolatières*, swizzle-sticks, wrappers and more. The "brown gold" of the Aztecs looks set to continue its conquest of the planet.

Jean Harlow in *Dinner at Eight* by George Cukor, 1935.

■ ADVERTISING
Talent in the service of chocolate

In the second half of the nineteenth century, great illlustrators such as Mucha, Gerbault and Carrey used their talents in the service of chocolate. Firmin Bouisset's poster of 1893, in which a small girl sporting plaits chalks "Avoid imitations" on a wall, was associated with the image of Menier* (it was aimed particularly at the rival and similarly named firm of Meunier). In 1905, Cappiello designed the original poster depicting a frisky young foal, later to become the emblem of Poulain* (which means foal in French).

Industrial manufacturers* supplied their distributors with advertising boards and dummy products made of cardboard, which they displayed in shop windows. These were soon replaced by brilliantly colored enamel panels, which were more durable and were thus suitable for use outside. Advertising was to produce a minor masterpiece in the miniature Morris column, a combined moneybox and distributor of miniature bars* of Menier chocolate, which is now a rare collector's item.

By the early twentieth century, advertising had diversified to include decorated chocolate boxes,* school blotting pads and exercise-book covers, colored lithographs (p. 46–47) and educational pictures for sticking in albums, all aimed at capturing the loyalty of young consumers and turning them into collectors. One of the most famous of these trademark images, used to promote Banania* chocolate powder, was the Senegalese soldier exclaiming in pidgin French "*Y'a bon Banania*", (mmm, Banania!) an outmoded colonialist image now replaced by a small child. Meanwhile, the bold design of the mauve cow on the Suchard* Milka tablet first appeared in 1972 and has not been replaced to this day.

Nowadays, in its attempts to seduce the adult market outside the prolific spending periods of Christmas and Easter,* advertisers of chocolate appeal to concepts such as luxury, fantasy and exoticism. For many years chocolate was reputed to be an aphrodisiac,* and advertising still maintains the link with sensuality: "all because the lady loves..." runs one famous slogan. Finally, tradition and proof of quality still inspire confidence: Lindt still displays the bust of its founder, while Poulain and Menier regularly reproduce their competition medals on their wrappings.

Miniature Morris column, moneybox and distributor for bars of Menier chocolate, 1948. Private collection.

"Avoid imitations." Advertising poster by Firmin Bouisset for Menier chocolate, 1893. Private collection.

■ Alcoholic drinks

Finding wines and spirits capable of accompanying chocolate without distorting its aroma is a fascinating quest. Possible partners can be found for chocolate in all its forms, only champagne remaining totally incompatible with it.

A square of milk chocolate* goes well with a sweet white wine such as a Riesling or a *vin de paille* from the Jura region of France, or with a slightly tannic red such as Saint Émilion. Milk chocolate desserts and combinations of chocolate and fruit (cherries, apricots, raspberries, etc.) are complemented by fruity wines such as a young Sauternes or a late-harvested Gewurztraminer.

Dark chocolate, with its higher content of cocoa, is more difficult, and impossible to marry with white wine. Only fine red wines, silky but with concentrated tannins, such as a great Châteauneuf-du-Pape or Côte-Rôtie, mellowed with age, will do. A chocolate bar* with a high cocoa content or a lightly sweetened bitter chocolate dessert makes a perfect partnership with naturally sweet wines such as Tokaji, Maury and Muscat, or with fortified wines, whose toasted aromas of dried fruit and spices bring out the full flavor of chocolate. Ten-year-old port, madeira and sherry all develop aromas of walnuts and almonds which make an agreeable complement to the bitterness of fine chocolate.* Finally, the complex aromas of spirits matured in wood—whether based on wine such as cognac or armagnac, on grain such as whisky, or on fruit—are marvelous with dark chocolate desserts. A twelve-year-old single malt whisky or a warm, amber-colored vintage rum makes a sublime accompaniment to a ganache.*

■ Aphrodisiac

Although the Aztec* king Montezuma always drank several cups* of chocolate before visiting his harem, it would appear that the drink's aphrodisiac qualities derived not so much from cacao as from the spices* such as pepper and chilli which it then also contained. And even though these were replaced in eighteenth-century Europe by vanilla and cinnamon, royal favorites continued to put their faith in the virtues of chocolate, indulging in excessive quantities as a stimulant, or offering it to their lovers to improve their performance. The Marquis de Sade, meanwhile, found himself imprisoned for poisoning young women with chocolate pastilles laced with Spanish fly to awaken their desires.

No modern scientific research has succeeded in demonstrating that the components of chocolate (cocoa and sugar) act as sexual stimulants. Reviving and anti-depressant though chocolate undoubtedly is, it cannot rightfully claim to possess aphrodisiac qualities. In our dreams, nevertheless, romance and chocolate will always go hand in hand.

Facing page:
Charles-Joseph
Natoire
(1700–1777),
*Portrait of
Mademoiselle
de Charolais*
(detail).
Musée national
du château
de Versailles.

"Happy chocolate, which having circled the globe through women's smiles, finds its death at their lips in a delectable, melting kiss."

Anthelme Brillat-Savarin, 1826.

■ AUSTRIA AND GERMANY

Drinking chocolate arrived in Austria via Italy* in about 1640. Monks who discovered a taste for the beverage ensured its spread throughout the Holy Roman Empire, notably in what is today Germany. On his return from Spain in 1713, Charles VI introduced it to his court in Vienna. From this grew the firmly established Viennese tradition of serving cups* of rich chocolate flavoured with sugar and vanilla and topped with a cloud of whipped cream (*Schlagsahne*) sprinkled with cocoa powder. The beverage also became popular in Germany.

But it was in the realm of *pâtisserie** that the Austrians surpassed themselves, producing the first recipe for a cake made with chocolate in 1778, and thus opening up a whole world of inspiration which has yet to be exhausted. In 1832, in response to Prince Klemens von Metternich's request for a 'dense, compact and masculine' dessert, his chief pâtissier,

Advertisement for Riquet chocolate.

Imperial Torte.

Franz Sacher, produced a rich chocolate cake sandwiched with a fine layer of apricot jelly and covered with chocolate fondant icing. Known henceforth as Sacher Torte, it was to become a great classic throughout the world.

In Vienna, authentic Sacher Torte may be savored at the Hôtel Sacher or the Pâtisserie Demel, both of which claim sole ownership of the original recipe. This remains a matter of some controversy, with one establishment placing the apricot jelly in the middle of the cake and the other under the icing. Another masterpiece of Austrian cuisine, Imperial Torte, alternates fine layers of milk chocolate* and almond paste. The great German classic, meanwhile, is Black Forest gateau, a confection of chocolate, whipped cream, cherries and kirsch.

The Austrians and Germans are also great consumers of chocolate in the form of small bars* or chocolates purchased individually.

◼ AZTECS
Food for the gods

Cultivated from the fourth to the ninth centuries by the Mayas, the cacao tree* became the focus of a veritable cult* among the Toltecs in the ninth to the twelfth centuries. To the Aztec civilization (twelfth to sixteenth centuries), it was one of the finest ornaments of paradise, the kingdom of the god

Quetzalcoatl.* Originally, these indigenous peoples ate only the refreshing, slightly acid pulp inside the pod, discarding the bitter seed, or beans,* within. No one knows who first had the idea of fermenting and roasting the beans, crushing them to make a paste,* then mixing the paste with spices,* diluting it with water and beating the mixture to a froth. As time went on, the Aztecs adopted chocolate as their nourishing staple drink. While their king drank pure chocolate from a golden goblet, the people made do with a chocolate-flavored maize broth (called *atolle*), drunk from dishes fashioned from tortoise shells.

The dried beans were also used as a form of currency. Four beans would buy a pumpkin, ten a rabbit, and a hundred a slave. It was a means of exchange that was also used for paying taxes: the province of Cihnatlan, for instance, paid 800 *cargas* to the king (a *carga* was 24,000 beans) twice a year. Shamans, meanwhile, prized the beans for their medicinal properties, using them to combat fatigue and diarrhoea, while cocoa butter served to make ointments for the treatment of wounds, burns and haemorrhoids (see Health).

Above:
Cacao tree.
Mexican codex,
second half of the
sixteenth century.

Banania tins
from *c.*1920
and *c.*1950.
Private collection.

◼ Banania

When, on a visit to Venezuela, a French pharmacist by the name of Pierre-François Lardet tasted a drink made from cocoa powder, sugar and banana flour, he immediately had the idea of bringing it back to Europe. On 31 August 1914, after several years devoted to perfecting the recipe and manufacture of the drink, he registered the trademark "Banania," the first enriched chocolate powder, which he launched using modern marketing techniques. Numerous other manufacturers launched similar products in an attempt to compete with Banania's success: in the 1920s, for instance, Félix Potin produced Banika, which was described as a "breakfast drink based on

cocoa and banana flour with added vitamins".

The recipe for Banania, now owned by an American consortium, has remained virtually unchanged to the present day, though a new enriched formula, with added vitamins and cereals, has been launched to appeal to a new generation of children—and their parents.

More nourishing than simple cocoa or chocolate powder,* enriched chocolate drinks still enjoy a considerable degree of confidence among mothers in both Europe and the United States, who see it as providing the guarantee of a nutritious and balanced, healthy breakfast for their children.

■ BARS
The pleasure of eating chocolate

Chocolate bars were familiar to the Aztecs.* In a work published in 1630, the missionary Thomas Gage reported that "the Indians put cocoa paste* on a palm leaf, and then put it in the shade where it hardens." For several centuries in Europe, drinking chocolate was made using fingers or wafers of cocoa paste. But even if these contained sugar and spices,* they could not be consumed as such. The English were the first, in 1674, to propose "fingers of chocolate in the Spanish fashion" intended for eating. These were soon followed by solid chocolate in other forms, such as pastilles. The chocolate bar as we know it today, designed to be easily broken into squares, appeared soon after the invention of the molding* process, in 1830, which made its production possible.

Curiously, the country that invented chocolate bars, Great Britain,* consumes fewer of them than any other country in Europe. Bars of 4 oz (100 g) are available throughout Europe, and in France* these account for 30 percent of production and 45 percent of consumption, with four million bars (50 percent milk chocolate* and 40 percent dark chocolate*) devoured daily. In the U.S., bar consumption has fluctuated in recent years, but one area clearly on the increase is funsize and snack size bars, whose sales grew by 12 percent from 1998 to 1999.

Chocolate bars come in many different varieties: plain, with hazelnuts or puffed rice, filled with praline* or almond paste, to name but a few. In 1993, Michel Chaudun of the company Weiss was the first to launch a bar containing slivers of roasted and crushed cocoa bean,* an idea adopted by many other master *chocolatiers* and industrial manufacturers. In response to the recent growth in popularity of chocolate with a high cocoa content and for the finest *grand cru* chocolate (see Varieties), "luxury" chocolate bars have also made their appearance, aimed at an essentially adult market.

Overleaf:
A selection of chocolate including tablets by the French master *chocolatiers* Voisin, Valrhona and Bonnat.

Bayonne

The first chocolate factory in France* was set up in Bayonne, following the arrival in the harbor of a sailing ship laden with a cargo of cocoa beans,* brought, according to legend, by an angel.

Tradition generally attributes the introduction of chocolate to France to Jewish chocolate-makers who settled in Bayonne in 1609, having been hounded out of first Spain and then Portugal.

In fact, the manufacture* of chocolate appears not to have existed in Bayonne before 1670, when, according to the town's archives, an alderman was required to "pay 25 *livres* for chocolate which he brought from Spain to give to persons of consequence." Not until 1687 do we find mention of a chocolate-maker in Bayonne. Whatever the date of their arrival, the Jewish chocolate-makers lived in the Saint-Esprit area, going to their clients' houses in the centre of town in order to make chocolate for them. They rapidly found themselves in competition with other chocolate makers in the town, who in 1691 obtained an injunction preventing Jews from selling chocolate to private customers within its walls.

In 1761, ten Bayonne chocolate-makers formed a corporation to protect their interests and impose controls on the sale of chocolate in the town. In response to this, the Jewish chocolate-makers took them to the parliament at Bordeaux, which found in their favor in 1767.

With the Revolution of 1789, and technical improvements, these problems smoothed themselves out. In the nineteenth century, the Bayonne chocolate industry reached its heyday; the tradition remains strong today in the Bayonne Chocolate Academy, with its guild of master *chocolatiers.** The town's specialty remains hot chocolate,* whipped into a froth before serving.

Claude-Joseph Vernet, *The Port of Bayonne*, 1761. Musée de la Marine, Paris.

■ BEANS
The secret of the cocoa pod

After harvesting, the fruit of the cacao tree* is split open and the seeds, or beans, and the surrounding pulp are removed. According to the customs of different countries, the beans and pulp are then either heaped in piles and covered with banana leaves, or put in wooden boxes holding between 90 to 220 pounds (40 to 100 kg). Natural yeasts in the air cause spontaneous fermentation of the whitish pulp, which in two days reaches a temperature of 113–122°F (45-50°C) and turns to liquid, draining out of holes in the boxes to be transformed into a delicious cocoa vinegar. This first fermentation is anaerobic, or oxygen-free, and the product is therefore alcoholic. Once the pulp has disappeared, the beans are turned regularly, allowing the air to circulate and oxygen to penetrate, so producing an acetic, or aerobic, fermentation.

This external transformation renders the walls of the bean cells permeable, producing a series of chemical reactions between the various elements they contain. Enzymes react with the proteins to produce the beginnings of aromas, and with certain polyphenols to produce compounds which oxidize to give the characteristic brown color of cocoa. The natural bitterness and astringency of the beans, meanwhile, is gradually reduced. The process takes three days for *criollo* beans and a week for other varieties;* any longer, and putrescent smells begin to appear. It is an essential and delicate stage in production which requires experience, and since the process cannot be fully controlled, the product can be of very variable quality; hence the attempts by chocolate manufacturers* to develop an industrially controlled process of fermentation.

After fermentation, the beans still contain 60 percent moisture, which must be reduced to 8 percent or less in order to ensure optimum conservation during storage and transportation. Two drying techniques exist, one natural, the other artificial. To dry naturally, the beans are spread out in the sun on the ground (p. 112), on cement floors, on wooden boards, on plastic sheets or on trestle tables. If it rains, sliding roofs are swiftly pulled across to cover them. This long and gradual drying process, which may last up to a fortnight, is sometimes accompanied by traditional ceremonies (see Cult). Artificial drying at 182°F (100°C) may be used as a complement or a substitute. In this, the beans are either placed on a heated surface or dried by hot air. If this quick but high-energy method is used, care must be taken not to let the beans come into contact with the gases, which would give them an unpleasant smoky flavor. Thorough drying avoids the formation of mold, which would spoil the cocoa butter,* and prevents over-fermentation. The dried beans are then checked and sorted, put in sacks and stored to await export or processing (see Cocoa paste).

"You need to taste cocoa beans in order to appreciate to the full the genius that men are capable of applying in their quest for pleasure."

James de Coquet, *Propos de table*, 1964.

Opening cocoa pods, Trinidad.

■ BELGIUM

For two centuries, Flanders was part of the immense Spanish empire. As early as the sixteenth century, it thus became one of the first European countries to taste the new cocoa-based drink. In the late seventeenth century, the first chocolate factories* were established in Brussels. It was to Jean Neuhaus,* *chocolatier* in the exclusive Galerie de la Reine shopping arcade, that Belgium owed the invention of the praline chocolate, in 1912, and of the protective cardboard packaging, the *ballotin*, in 1915.

Belgian praline chocolates are generally molded:* the liquid chocolate is poured into a mold to form a shell, and when this has been filled, the base is sealed with a layer of chocolate. Among the innumerable varieties available, four have achieved the status of classics: praline in a milk chocolate* shell; *crème fraiche* or butter in a dark chocolate* shell, known as fondant;

marzipan in chocolate fondant; and, most celebrated of all, the Manon. Garnished with a walnut and *crème fraiche* or butter, the Manon is encased in white chocolate or fondant sugar icing and is sometimes flavoured with coffee* (and therefore does not contain the slightest suggestion of cacao!).

Belgian praline chocolates are made in enormous quantities and distributed throughout the world by the major chocolate companies: Godiva, Guylian, Leonidas and Neuhaus. Two-thirds of total production (comprising 83 varieties) is by Leonidas, founded in 1913 and now with 1,750 franchise outlets worldwide. Godiva, established in 1946, exports 50 percent of its Belgian production and also has factories in Tokyo and New York. Guylian, meanwhile, produces 75 tons of chocolates daily, sold in 140 countries.

Two-thirds of the coating chocolate (see Confectioners' coating) produced in Belgium is exported. Barry-Callebaut and Kraft-Jacobs are the two giants of the European chocolate industry. The Belgians consume an annual average of 16 pounds (7.3 kg) of chocolate per head of population, a relatively modest figure when set against the amount they produce.

Advertisement for
Côte d'Or chocolate, 1937.

Grinding cocoa beans,
Godiva factory, Brussels.

Brillat-Savarin (Anthelme)

Lawyer, deputy to the Constituent Assembly and finally a magistrate, Brillat-Savarin (1755–1826) was a gourmet who delighted in organizing gastronomic dinners at his house, creating some of the dishes himself. In 1826, he published his celebrated *Physiologie du goût* (*Physiology of Taste*), a series of "gastronomic meditations" in conversational style, spiced with aphorisms and anecdotes. He included advice on the successful preparation of hot chocolate,* as revealed to him by Madame d'Arestrel, Mother Superior of the Convent of the Visitation in Belley: "... it is sufficient to prepare it the evening before in a ceramic coffee pot and to leave it. The night's rest concentrates it and gives it a velvety smoothness which makes it much better."

Anthelme Brillat-Savarin. Engraving by Lambert, early nineteenth century.

Brillat-Savarin loved chocolate in all its forms: "[it] is delectable in creams, [it] delights us still late in the evening in ices, croquettes and drawing-room sweetmeats, not to mention the pleasant diversions of pastilles and *diablotins*."

He also detailed the beneficial effects of Debauve's chocolate flavored with ambergris.

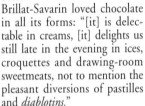

"Any man who has drunk too deeply of the cup of pleasure. Any man who has devoted to work a notable part of the time intended for sleep. Any man of wit who finds himself temporarily a dullard. Any man tormented by an idée-fixe which destroys his liberty of thought. Let all these take a good half-litre of amber-flavored chocolate, which I name the chocolate of the afflicted."

Anthelme Brillat-Savarin, 1826.

Cacao tree

Cultivated by the Mayas and the Aztecs,* the cacao tree came originally from the great Amazonian rainforest. It was first called *Amygdala pecunaria* by botanists, before being rechristened in 1735 by Linnaeus, the father of zoology, who named it *Theobroma cacao*, or "food of the gods," an allusion to the cult* with which the Indians surrounded it. It requires a hot (77–86ºF, 25–30ºC), humid climate, growing in a band of latitude 20 degrees north and 20 degrees south of the equator (see Plantation).

A member of the genus *Sterculaceae*, the cacao tree grows straight and slender, with few

Cocoa pods and beans.

branches, to a height of between 39 and 49 feet (12 and 15 m) in the wild: in cultivation, it is kept to between 13 and 33 feet (4 and 10 m). As the equatorial and tropical regions have no true winter, the cacao tree bears flowers and fruit constantly and simultaneously. Its leaves are broad, oblong and pointed, and the flowers grow in clusters from the main branches and the trunk. White or pale yellow flushed with pink, they have no perfume, and are tiny (some under half an inch across) in comparison with the fruit. The fruit, known as a pod, is like a small rugby ball in shape, and is attached to the trunk or branches by a short stalk. Each pod contains 25 to 75 seeds (or beans*), enveloped in a whitish pulp which is both sweet and slightly acid.

There are three different botanical species of cacao tree, the *criollo*, the *forastero* and the *trinitario*, each bearing pods of a highly distinctive color, size and shape. The long, striated shape of the *criollo* pod was the inspiration for the first Coca-Cola bottles.

"The cocoa bean is a phenomenon which nature has never repeated.
Never have so many qualities been brought together in so small a fruit."
Alexander von Humboldt (1769–1859).

Giandujotti
by Caffarel.

Caffarel

Having previously "Italianized" it, Paolo Caffarelli (1783–1845) used his original French name for the chocolate factory* that he opened in Turin in 1826 (see Italy). He rapidly acquired a reputation throughout the Piedmont region of Italy for his "health-giving cinnamon-flavored chocolate," recommended for the whole family, as well as for his pioneering use in Italy of hydraulic power and steam-driven machinery. His son, Isidore Caffarel (1817–1867) invented the *gianduja*, a small ingot-shaped chocolate (originally without milk*), filled with a smooth paste made from Piedmont hazelnuts (undoubtedly the best). The name *giandujotti* was taken from a hero of the struggle for Italian independence nicknamed Gian d'la Duja ('John the Jug') because of his predilection for wine: during Carnival celebrations in 1865, he distributed Caffarel's delicious creations liberally to the crowd and "authorized" them to be called *giandujotti*.

Today Caffarel remains one of the largest chocolate manufacturers in Piedmont, with specialties distinguished by their sophistication in both form and flavor (see Design).

Chocolate box

Tin biscuit boxes decorated with lithographs first made their appearance in Great Britain* in 1868. In France,* the biscuit manufacturer Lu and the chocolate manufacturer Menier were the first to follow suit, using this utilitarian object to distinguish their own products from the competition, attracting clients and keeping their business. These boxes and tins were too pretty to throw away: gentlemen kept their nails in them and ladies their haberdashery or special treats for the children. Banania* even went so far as to print labels saying "flour", "sugar" and "pasta" on its famous yellow tins of chocolate powder.

The firm Chocolat de Royat, founded in 1898 and later renamed Marquise de Sévigné, was the first to launch luxury cardboard boxes, richly decorated with fabrics or paintings,

which are now collector's items (see Collecting). Jean Neuhaus,* who invented praline chocolates in 1912, also created the *ballotin*, a small cardboard box designed to hold an assortment of chocolates selected individually.

Decorative boxes of chocolates,* a luxury between the wars, are now a prominent feature of shop displays at Christmas time. Chocolate assortments are beautifully presented and distinguished by brightly colored foil wrappings, while the boxes are decorated with reproductions of paintings, picture-postcard landscapes or appealing baby animals. Before the proliferation of such images, it was not unknown for customers to frame the lids of chocolate boxes to decorate their walls.

Master *chocolatiers* accord great importance to the aesthetic qualities of their packaging. Some even employ the talents of fashion* designers: Robert Linxe commissioned the Hermes house designer to create the prestigious boxes for La Maison du Chocolat.

Chocolate boxes from the *Marquise de Sévigné* catalog, 1928. Private collection.

45

Chocolate houses

Chocolate houses sprang up in London in the mid-seventeenth century, serving hot chocolate* made with milk rather than water, and frequently fortified with an egg or a finger of madeira. They also served beer and coffee. In these elegant and reputedly seditious establishments, open to men and women alike, members gathered to play cards and dice, to gamble, to obtain theatre tickets and listen to music, and above all to discuss politics or affairs of the heart. The most famous was White's, which opened in St James's in 1697. In 1746, the Cocoa-Tree Club became the haunt of politicians, particularly Tories, who met there on the pretext of taking chocolate in order to hatch political plots. After 1750, only the more modest establishments survived, frequented by the public at large. The most select chocolate houses became private clubs, strictly limited to gentlemen from the ranks of high society. The chocolate house had no equivalent in the German-speaking nations (see Austria and Germany), but some of the large cafes, notably in Leipzig, set aside a room, the *Shokoladestube*, for devotees of chocolate. In other European countries, establishments offering hot drinks served mainly coffee and tea, and more rarely chocolate.

The situation remains virtually unchanged to these days,

White's chocolate house, London, 1708. Colored lithograph published by Cadbury.

although a number of *salons de thé* throughout Europe have nevertheless forged a reputation on the basis of their delicious hot chocolate.

■ Chocolates

Chocolate pastilles have existed since the late seventeenth century, and filled chocolate cases since 1912. Made in perfect bite-sized pieces, individual chocolates are designed to be popped in the mouth in one go. "A chocolate is a filling to be coated or a hollow case to be filled," wrote the *pâtissier* Gaston Lenôtre. The filling to be coated (ganache,* praline,* almond paste, etc.) may be stamped mechanically before being wrapped in a stream of liquid chocolate. Alternatively,

it may be plunged into coating chocolate (see Confectioners' coating), a time-consuming process carried out by hand by master *chocolatiers.*

The hollow case to be filled is frequently a molded* Belgian praline (see Belgium), their thick coating melting more slowly in the mouth. The best chocolates have the finest quality coating, stimulating the taste buds with its flavor before yielding to the charms of the filling. Master *chocolatiers* use considerable ingenuity to vary the shape and decoration of their creations (see Design). Among the products made by industrial chocolate companies, praline-filled *rochers* remain one of the most popular.

Overleaf:
A sumptuous selection of chocolates.

■ Chocolatière

In the Spanish monasteries of the New World, chocolate was prepared in a pot-bellied or pear-shaped utensil, made of terracotta or plated copper in order to retain the heat. Following the Aztec* custom, the chocolate was beaten to a froth with a carved wooden stick with a ridged end, known as a *moulinet* or *molinillo*.

In the seventeenth century, a sweeter recipe for chocolate spread throughout Spain*, bringing in its wake a fashion for more elegant vessels from which to pour a beverage which was now the delight of Spanish ladies.

Tin and pewter, commonly used up to that point, were now replaced by materials more fitting for aristocratic tables, such as silver, enamel and porcelain, while Chinese and later Japanese craftsmen produced pots for chocolate as well as for coffee in response to the new demand. A horizontal handle in some precious wood protected fingers against burns. The spout, meanwhile, was placed in the upper part of the vessel in order to retain the sediment inside, and a hole in the middle of the lid accommodated a boxwood swizzle-stick. Usually the *chocolatière* was raised on three feet in order to allow a small plate-warmer to be slipped underneath. The earliest known silver *chocolatière* was presented to Louis XIV by the Siamese ambassador in 1686. Those

Copper *chocolatière*, eighteenth century. Private collection.

Silver *chocolatière* in the form of a cocoa pod, *c.*1930. Private collection.

most commonly found today date from the mid-eighteenth century.

A *chocolatière* was one of the prerogatives of high society, and for Madame de Sévigné (see Literature), it was quite impossible to envisage life without one. Fine porcelain services began to appear in the eighteenth century, the first being made at Sèvres in 1784. With the appearance of finely ground cocoa powder* in the late nineteenth century, *chocolatières* lost their feet, along with the warmers they sheltered. These precious pieces, frequently depicted in paintings,* are now extremely valuable.

Church

The missionaries who accompanied the conquistadors were ambivalent in their attitude towards the drinking of chocolate, considering that it "led to sins of the flesh" while at the same time applauding the morality of a beverage which was not intoxicating.

To the religious community, chocolate was useful above all as a restorative during ritual fasting. The prickly question then arose as to whether chocolate should be considered a food or a drink. The matter was put to Pope Pius V, who in 1569 ruled that chocolate made with water might be consumed without breaking the fast. But after his death the problem resurfaced, causing great agitation among religious orders, who exchanged virulent diatribes on the subject for nearly a century to come. Finally, in 1664, Cardinal Francesco Maria Brancaccio settled the matter, declaring: "Drinks do not break fasting. Wine, nourishing though it is, does not break the fast. The same is true of chocolate. That it is nourishing is undeniable, but it does not follow that it is a food."

Spanish settlers in Mexico (see Spain) in the seventeenth century developed a passion for chocolate, drinking it every two hours even during religious services, during which it was brought to them by their serving women, to the great scandal of the priests.

Dom Bernard de Salazar, Bishop of Chiappa, found these comings and goings during mass intolerable, and threatened to excommunicate anyone consuming chocolate during divine service. The reaction was vengeful: the bishop died by

poison—administered to him in his chocolate. Cacao swiftly regained its odor of sanctity, however, and in 1743 Pope Benedict XIV was known to freely present chocolate pastilles to the officers of his guard. From the nineteenth century, chocolate even forged links with the great Christian festivals of Christmas and Easter.*

Dom Bernard de Salazar in the Region of Chiappa. Illustration from the New Survey of the West Indies *by Thomas Gage, c.1640.*

Club

Over the last twenty years, the vogue for comparative tastings has engendered the birth of clubs for chocolate enthusiasts. In France,* the *Club des croqueurs de chocolat* (Chocolate Crunchers' Club), formerly the *Club des cinglés du chocolat* (Chocolate Nuts), was founded in 1980. With a membership strictly limited to 150, it very rarely accepts new members. Six times a year, it holds blind comparative tastings in Paris, in which different chocolates and chocolate products are discussed and accorded grades. In the United States you could join the Heavenly Chocolate Club, which dispatches gourmet chocolate selections to members on a monthly basis. Also worth mentioning are

Overleaf: Cocoa butter and mass.

Milka chocolate by Suchard. Advertisement from *L'Illustration*, May 1912. Private collection.

numerous internet clubs allowing consumers ever-greater access to their favorite candies, such as the Chocosphere Club (www.chocosphere.com).

In Great Britain,* the Chocolate Society (created in 1991) and the Chocolate Club (1994) provide their members with information on the world of chocolate, as well as offering them the opportunity to buy selected products. There are chocolate clubs in countries all over the world: Italy has a Chocolate Confraternity, Germany has a website dedicated to the Milka cow as well as a well-supported Fair Trade Society, *Transfair,* selling chocolate. Buying fair trade chocolate via associations is a good way of ensuring a fair deal for the Third World farmers who produce cocoa beans.

Cocoa butter

In 1825, an Amsterdam chocolate-manufacturer by the name of Coenraad Van Houten perfected a process for extracting cocoa butter* from cocoa paste.* This involves subjecting the paste to great pressure under hydraulic presses, with the resulting butter then being filtered and deodorized. Once refined, it is then smoothed, or "conched," to give it a homogeneous, brittle appearance. The dry residue left in the press after the cocoa butter has been extracted is known as cocoa "cake". This is pulverized to make cocoa powder.*

In 1591, Juan de Cardenas described the "oily layer floating on the surface of the chocolate," "greasy and unctuous" to the taste, as "soft, soothing and amorous!" The Mayas used this "golden-colored oil" with its healing properties (see Health) to protect themselves from the burning rays of the sun. Cocoa butter is still a common ingredient of pharmaceutical and cosmetic products, where it is useful as it rarely goes rancid.

Cocoa butter plays an essential part in the manufacture of chocolate, being added to the cocoa paste to supplement its natural cocoa butter content (see Manufacturing process) to make it smoother and glossier, and to make confectioners' coating* easier to mold (see Molding). Belgian praline chocolates (see Belgium) owe their special rich smoothness to their extremely high cocoa butter content. Cocoa butter is also one of the principal ingredients of white chocolate.*

The high cost of cocoa butter, however, has prompted some European countries to seek to replace it with a proportion of vegetable fat, a practice which has now become the object of a new European regulation.* Producer countries such as the Ivory Coast have launched a program to encourage cultivation of the shea tree to provide an alternative source of vegetable fat for use in chocolate, hoping thereby to avoid the slump in their economy that a reduction in cocoa butter exports to the West will inevitably bring.

■ Coffee

Whether in ganache* or *pâtisserie*,* coffee always makes a sublime accompaniment to chocolate, with flavors combining in a marriage of melting passion. It is a partnership confirmed countless times daily: in France* alone, over 350 million *napolitains* are consumed annually with a *petit noir*, or strong black coffee. Placed on the tongue, these small square or rectangular wafers of dark chocolate* hold a sensory delight in store, the contrast of liquid and solid, hot and cold, culminating as the chocolate liquefies into a melting smoothness. The Italians—creators of a cream-filled chocolate to melt in their coffee—also boast a beverage known as *bicerin*, prepared with equal parts of coffee, chocolate and cream (see Italy).

Which coffee to choose? The liveliest and least acid, such as mochas from Ethiopia and Brazil, and Venezuelan and Jamaican varieties (especially Blue Mountain), offer a particularly satisfying combination of aromas to the palate. The perfect union is achieved with Java Boengi, which is blessed with a natural flavor of chocolate.

This widely-reputed complicity between the two beverages, coffee and cocoa, can be attributed in part to striking similarities between the two: both appeared in Europe at about the same time; the cacao tree* and the coffee shrub flourish in similar conditions (see Plantation); coffee, like cocoa, receives its first treatment (extraction, washing and drying) in the place of harvesting; and the process of roasting that enables both coffee and cocoa to release their full flavor.

Collecting

Silver *chocolatières* and chocolate services, chocolate boxes* decorated with colored lithographs and enamel panels, period wrappings and advertising materials—all are now sought after by collectors, if they have not already entered museum collections. The Industrial Revolution, which brought about the democratization of chocolate, went hand in hand with the growth of advertising.* In France,* Aristide Boucicaut was the first to conceive the idea of offering pictures to children shopping with their mothers at the well-known Paris store Bon Marché. These colorful images, often with details picked out in gold, owed their brilliance to the process of color lithography. In 1884, Poulain* took up the idea for its "vanilla cream breakfast," to such resounding success that the company set up its own printing works within its factory. Here, 350,000 colored lithographs were produced in 1900. The majority of chocolate manufacturers employed the same technique of seduction, and these images, and the albums into which they were pasted, now constitute a rich source of information for collectors on daily life in the late nineteenth century.

Chocolate also has a place in the field of philately. The stamps of cocoa-producing countries naturally feature the crop (see Cultivation) which is frequently a principal export and therefore vital for the national economy. Africa, one of the most prominent producers worldwide from the beginning of the century, has produced some exceptionally fine examples, dazzling in their use of color. Some are veritable

lessons in natural history, showing cacao trees* and pods, often split in two to show the beans;* others show scenes of cultivation, harvesting and drying. The most interesting stamps to date have been issued by Cameroon, the Ivory Coast, Gabon, Ghana and Togo.

■ CONFECTIONERS' COATING
Enrobing, molding, icing, decorating

The manufacture of semi-prepared products, such as cocoa powder,* cocoa butter* and coating chocolate, or confectioners' coating as it is more properly called, represents one of the two principal activities of the chocolate industry (the other being the fabrication of finished products, see Factories). In terms of volume, the most significant activity is the production of confectioners' coating, hence the generic label "suppliers of confectioners' coating" applied to all manufacturers of semi-prepared chocolate products.

Confectioners' coating (whether of milk* or dark chocolate*) is required to conform to certain standards, which in Europe lay down that it must have a vegetable fat (i.e. cocoa butter) content of a minimum of 31 percent. Cocoa butter is the ingredient that makes the finished product smooth, glossy and

easy to work: the higher the content of cocoa butter, the more easily the chocolate melts in the mouth.

The primary ingredient in the work of both industrial manufacturers and master *chocolatiers** alike, confectioners' coating is also essential to *pâtissiers* and other confectioners, who use it to enrobe, mold, glaze and otherwise decorate their chocolate creations. The Barry Callebaut group (a subsidiary of the company Klaus J. Jacobs Holdings), the product of a merger between two major chocolate manufacturers, is today the world leader in the processing of cocoa beans and the production of chocolate. The company offers a choice of over a thousand different chocolate recipes, to industrial biscuit, ice cream and chocolate manufacturers as well as to master bakers, *pâtissiers* and *chocolatiers* and restaurants throughout the world. In 1925, Charles Callebaut first conceived the idea of liquid chocolate, and now 70 percent of confectioners' coating is supplied in this form.

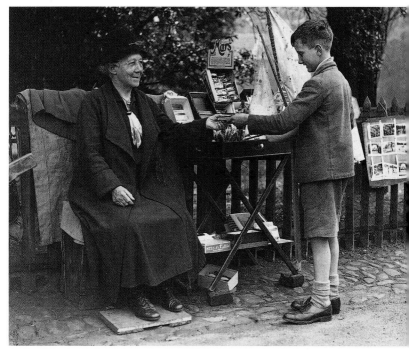

■ Confectionery

Chocolate confectionery comprises molded shells (such as Easter* eggs and Christmas figures) and all fillings (biscuit, praline, almond paste and so forth) covered with a chocolate confectioners' coating.* The world's most popular form of confectionery is the tablet of chocolate,* born of the simple notion, conceived in the early twentieth century, that a bar could be divided into individual sections. In 1920, the American Frank Mars invented the bar named after him, consisting of a nougat and caramel filling encased in chocolate. Included as part of standard G.I. rations (see Iron rations) during the Second World War, the Mars Bar has travelled throughout the world: it still tops the sales charts in a market worth over $14 billion annually in the United States alone.

A practical, high-energy snack,* easily fitted into the pocket, the chocolate bar and other similar snack products are emblematic of the modern age. The development of this sector (which has grown by 50 percent in the last decade) is largely responsible for the recent leap in chocolate consumption.* It now accounts for over half the European chocolate market.

The British and American markets have now virtually abandoned chocolate in tablet form in favor of milk chocolate confectionery, of which they are the most avid consumers in the world. The most successful of these products—Mars, Kit-Kat, Smarties, and other household names in confectionery—are Anglo-Saxon in origin. Continental Europeans, on the other hand, retain their preference for chocolate in tablet form.

Mrs Weelabread, nicknamed "the chocolate lady," selling Mars Bars in Kensington Gardens in London, c.1930.

Facing top: Colored lithograph printed by Poulain, c.1900. Private collection.

Facing bottom: Confectioners' coating being poured into moulds, Barry Callebaut factory.

Consumption

In Mexico and the West Indies, cocoa in the form of "cakes" or "rolls" is traditionally used as a spice in cooking, but chocolate is rarely eaten. The map of world chocolate consumption presents the reverse image of that of chocolate production.* There are two reasons for this. Firstly, the producers are generally developing countries, where the average income does not allow the purchase of chocolate. Secondly, the hot and humid equatorial climate in which the cacao tree flourishes renders conservation* of the finished product difficult.

The Swiss and the British lead the world in chocolate consumption (roughly 22 pounds or 9.8–10 kg annually per head of population), but in fact British consumption is probably higher because the Swiss figure does not take into account "exports" by tourists. Americans eat a relatively modest 10 pounds (4.6 kg) per head annually. Over the past decade, consumption generally has increased by 50 percent (see Confectionery), with the greatest volume of sales at Easter* and Christmas. Finally, it is possible that increasingly sweet tastes in Asia, particularly in Japan and China, will modify the map of world consumption in the future.

Cortés (Hernán)

On 21 April 1519, Cortés (1485–1547) landed on the Tabasco coast, west of Yucatán, having sailed from Cuba with a fleet of eleven ships carrying 508 soldiers. After receiving a peaceful welcome from the emissaries of the Aztec* king, Montezuma, he nevertheless decided to conquer the capital by force of arms. The native people, who had never before seen either cannon or horses, offered little resistance, and in November Montezuma capitulated. Convinced that Cortés was the reincarnation of the god Quetzalcoatl,* whose return at this time had been predicted by the oracles, the king declared to him: "Here you shall find everything necessary for yourself and your followers, for here you are at home in your native land." The

conquistador took care not to disillusion him, allowing himself to be heaped with gold and precious stones, gifts from the Aztec people to their god. He was given apartments in the royal palace, and also received a 20,000 square foot plantation* of cacao trees*.

After imposing Spanish rule on the entire region, Cortés returned to Spain* in 1528, taking with him a cargo of cocoa beans* and utensils for making chocolate, and the jealously guarded secret of making the precious drink.

Facing page: Woman selling rolls of cocoa in a market, Trinidad.

Miguel González, *Montezuma receiving Hernán Cortés* (detail), 1698.

Cult

The Aztecs* marked the various stages of the cultivation* of the cacao tree* with ritual celebrations. In 1576, Garcia de Palacios recounted how before the cacao seeds were planted, the best beans* were exposed to the rays of the moon for four nights, during which time the men had to abstain from sexual intercourse. On the fifth day, when the seeds were planted, the bravest and strongest among them were permitted to rejoin the women. Thirteen days before the harvest, the men were again forbidden to visit the women; the picking of the pods was then accompanied by orgies.

The completion of the harvest was marked by celebrations, as described by Gonzalo Fernandez de Oviedo in 1530: "The effigy of the god 'Cacaguat' was hoisted up on a pole. To the top was attached a revolving frame, and to this 'bird-children' were tied by ropes. At a given signal, these flung themselves into the void, spinning through the air until they touched the ground to the jubilation of the people. Around the pole danced sixty men, their heads adorned with headdresses of multi-colored feathers, their bodies naked or painted, and some of them disguised as women. They were accompanied by musicians and a group of ten singers." The annual celebrations in honor of Ek Chuah, god of merchants and cocoa, were marked by the sacrifice of a white dog with cocoa-colored markings. In some Latin American countries, cocoa beans are still used as ritual gifts between betrothed couples or as offerings to the dead. In Ecuador, the drying process is sometimes accompanied by a cocoa dance, in which the Indians dance round the drying beans, turning them as they glow red in the sun. At Corpus Christi in Venezuela, men disguised as devils lie on the empty drying ground, while a priest bearing the holy sacrament steps over them.

In Europe and the U.S., chocolate is associated with Easter* and Christmas.

Harvesting cocoa pods, Cameroon.

Diego Rivera, *Offerings of Fruit, Tobacco, Cocoa and Vanilla being presented to the Emperor,* 1920–50. Mural fresco. Palacio nacional, Mexico City.

■ CULTIVATION: IN THE SHADE OF BANANA TREES

Cacao trees* are sown in nurseries and transplanted at the age of two years to plantations cleared from the rainforest. A distance of at least 8 feet (2.5 m) is left between them and, as they need shade in order to grow, other trees are planted at the same time to provide protection from wind, rain and, above all, direct sun. Lemon trees and banana trees may both fulfil this role of "parasol', but many planters prefer to use erythrina, dubbed the "mother of cocoa', which, thanks to its rapid growth and dense vegetation, provides effective shelter more rapidly.

At the age of seven or eight years, if it has manged to escape insect pests and cryptogamic or viral diseases, the cacao tree starts to become productive. Throughout the year, between 3,500 and 6,000 small flowers grow direct from the trunk, but only one in every hundred will be successfully pollinated by insects. A mere ten or twenty flowers per tree will produce fruit known as "pods," also growing direct from the trunk or one of the main branches.

Planters have to protect the pods from the attentions of monkeys, squirrels and above all rats, which love the sweet and slightly acid pulp surrounding the beans.* The pods are like small rugby balls in shape, and may weigh from 14 to 35 ounces (0.4–1 kg) according to the variety. Planters know they are ripe by their change in color (from green to red or red to orange), and can estimate their yield by tapping them with a finger. In many producer countries, the main harvests take place between November and January and May and July, but in very humid regions the harvest continues throughout the year. The implements used—machetes or "cocoa blades'—must be wielded with great skill in order not to damage the tree or neighboring flowers or buds. Each pod contains between forty and fifty beans, arranged in five densely packed rows around a placenta and enveloped in a whitish pulp. A fresh bean, resembling a rounded almond, weighs roughly a tenth of an ounce (2.5–3.5 g), which reduces by half as it dries: twenty pods, or half the annual yield of a cacao tree, are required to produce 35 ounces (1 kg) of usable beans.

CUP

Cup

When Cortés* first tasted chocolate, it was presented to him by King Montezuma in a golden cup. By the late seventeenth century, cups for the taking of this fashionable beverage appeared alongside *chocolatières** in Spain.* At the instigation of the Marquis de Mancera, viceroy of "New Spain" (Peru), the *mancerina* or *trembleuse* was invented: a special cup which fitted into a hollow cradle attached to the saucer, thus preventing it from slipping. This had the advantage of protecting the drinker from

Mancerina, or *trembleuse*, 1750. Porcelain. Museu de Ceramica, Barcelona.

the danger of spilling the frothy chocolate while stirring it, or while indulging in the practice of pouring a little out to cool and sipping it direct from the saucer.

Porcelain from China was to remain unrivalled in elegance and delicacy until 1710, when the Meissen porcelain factory in Saxony produced a tall cup without a handle.

During the eighteenth century sumptuous chocolate services were manufactured, the loveliest and most prestigious being produced in France by the royal porcelain factory at Sèvres.

■ DARK CHOCOLATE: BITTER DELIGHT

The first eating chocolate in solid form, invented in Great Britain* in 1674, was composed of dark chocolate. Its place was usurped by milk chocolate,* developed in Switzerland* in 1875. Although dark chocolate is still only in second place in the league table of world consumption,* it has nevertheless enjoyed a marked growth in popularity over the last decade.

This tendency towards increasingly bitter chocolate has its origins in the dramatic fall in cocoa prices in the years around 1985. As milk powder became proportionately more expensive, so manufacturers encouraged their customers to buy dark chocolate. The creative efforts of master *chocolatiers** in their quest for new aromas and in the encouragement of appreciation of *grands crus* (see Varieties) has also indisputably played a part in this evolution in taste.

Although the regulations* in force require a minimum of only 43 percent cacao content for high-quality chocolate, many dark chocolate bars* now available contain considerably more. This preference for a high percentage of cocoa is sometimes motivated by snobbery, however. Although it is frequently synonymous with an intensity of flavor appreciated by adults, it is nevertheless not a guarantee of quality. Indeed, certain bars with a cocoa content of over 70 percent are sometimes made from beans* that are too acid or have been badly roasted (see Manufacturing process).

Having found their preferred chocolate, ideal in its degree of strength, the balance of its varieties and its smoothness, true chocolate-lovers will remain faithful to it. The element of bitterness should be tempered in order to respect the harmony of flavors and the personality of the beans. Be wary, too, of chocolate that is *too* dark: a good dark chocolate should be a deep mahogany color, sometimes even tinged with russet.

Chocolates by
Michel Richart.

Facing page:
Wrapping from
a *Cocorico*
chocolate bar.
Private collection.

Design

In 1908, the Swiss Jean Tobler (see Switzerland) invented Toblerone, a chocolate bar with almond-and-honey nougat, molded in triangular sections recalling the mountains of his native land. This unusual and distinctive design remains one of Toblerone's principal assets. While chocolate bars* in tablet form are traditionally rectangular in shape and divided into squares, some are distinguished by motifs in relief featuring geometrical designs, drawings of hazelnuts, company trademarks and so on. In 1996, Yves Thuriès created chocolate bars mingling dark* and milk chocolate* to give a marbled effect.

In the world of chocolates,* each manufacturer has developed a particular range of shapes and decorative devices by which his product can be identified. Only a few varieties, such as *palets d'or*, truffles* and *rochers*, correspond to an unvarying shape. As in the world of fashion,* chocolate changes its inspiration according to the season: Christmas, St Valentine's Day, Easter* and even Mothers' Day are all opportunities to launch new collections, to be closely scrutinized and appraised in the gastronomic press.

In France,* Michel Richart, a designer before he took over the running of the family chocolate firm, has opened an innovative chain of shops called *Design et chocolat*. In his view, design and the quest for aesthetic perfection are inextricably linked with epicurean pleasure. Tiny Japanese-inspired chocolates, pyramids and *trompe-l'oeil* eggs are only a few examples of this modern art of chocolate. The Maison du Chocolat, meanwhile, has sought to create a more masculine image with the production of chocolates in the form of cigars. The *École des métiers de la table* in Paris has demonstrated its awareness of the fact that aesthetic considerations are becoming ever important in the fabrication of fine chocolate by including design as a compulsory part of its curriculum. Attractive presentation (see Chocolate box), whether or not it makes conscious reference to luxury, also plays its part in seducing potential customers. Playing on this fact, some chocolate manufacturers have employed the talents of specialized designers to strengthen their image.

> "I lost my head one day for some pavés of dark chocolate bristling with scorched hazelnuts, for a rocher filled with orange peel, for chocolate bars shivered with a hammer and sheathed in almonds and pistachios, for a praline chou covered in dark chocolate.'"
> Sonia Rykiel

▦ DRUG: AN ADDICTIVE TASTE

People frequently confess, in a rueful tone accompanied by a blissful smile, that they are addicted to chocolate. This is pure hyperbole, of course, since by definition an addictive drug must be capable of creating a dependence, which is not the case with chocolate: even an "addict" does not need constantly to increase his or her intake in order to experience the same degree of pleasure, and may be deprived of it altogether without suffering withdrawal symptoms. The discovery of the presence in cocoa of anandamide—also present in cannabis—was seized upon by some as an explanation of possible dependence on chocolate; for this substance to have any effect, however, a subject weighing 132 pounds (60 kg) would have to consume no less than 24 pounds (11 kg) of chocolate daily!

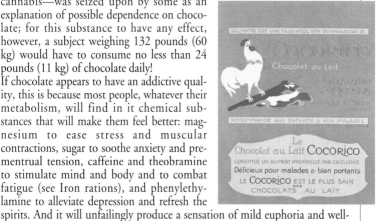

If chocolate appears to have an addictive quality, this is because most people, whatever their metabolism, will find in it chemical substances that will make them feel better: magnesium to ease stress and muscular contractions, sugar to soothe anxiety and pre-mentrual tension, caffeine and theobramine to stimulate mind and body and to combat fatigue (see Iron rations), and phenylethylamine to alleviate depression and refresh the spirits. And it will unfailingly produce a sensation of mild euphoria and well-being, as the very act of tasting it encourages the secretion of endorphins, a form of morphine produced by the body. Tortured souls could do much worse than resort to chocolate to relieve their solitude or their anxieties.

People who consume large amounts of chocolate—4 to 20 ounces (100–500 g) daily—generally display a perfectly normal psychological profile: they are often active and lively. In short, people who occasionally feel the need for a gentle lift and who unashamedly enjoy the good things in life.

▦ Easter

According to a legend going back to the eighth century, during Holy Week, church bells would fall silent and set off for Rome. On their return, on Easter Sunday, they would bring back with them thousands of eggs which they scattered in fields and gardens. In the fifteenth century, it became the custom to preserve eggs during Lent, when Christians were not supposed to eat meat, and to decorate them before hiding them among bushes and in the fields; on Easter morning, the children would set off

delightedly in search of them. The folklore of Easter varied from place to place, and in some regions the eggs were supposedly laid by hares on Easter morning! Over the years, the Lenten fast became less strictly observed and the eggs turned to chocolate; and in about 1830, with the mastery of the technique of tempering and the development of molding,* came the advent of Easter bunnies and the like.

Easter chocolate figures appear in many different forms, whether religious in theme (Easter lambs, bells, eggs or fish) or secular (bunnies, chicks and so forth). But eggs remain the universal symbol of Easter. Frequently they are tied with a satin bow, a tradition which goes back to the reign of Charlemagne: from that time until the reign of Louis XVI, the largest egg laid in France during Holy Week was tied with a red bow and presented to the king. As a change from three-dimensional eggs, the chocolate-manufacturer Michel Richart has launched a collection of *trompe-l'oeil* eggs traced on wafers of fine chocolate (see Design).

◾ Etymology

The word "cacao," which first appears in botanical writings in 1605, is derived from the Aztec* word *cacahuatl*, meaning the substance extracted from the cocoa bean.* The Spanish word for the cacao pod was *cabeza*, meaning "head," a term coined by the Spanish conquistadors, who fancied

Mexican Indian woman pouring chocolate. Codex, sixteenth century.

that the fruit of the cacao tree* resembled the shape of Amerindian skulls (indeed it was the custom among the Amerindians to massage the heads of newborn infants, in order to give them an oblong shape which was considered attractive).

"Chocolate" is a more or less phonetic transcription of the Mayan word *xocoatl*, pronounced "chocoatl." The etymology of this term remains a matter of considerable controversy, however. The hypothesis proposed by Thomas Gage in 1676 was for many years accepted as authoritative: according to him, *chocoatl* was a contraction of *atl*, or "water," and *choco*, an onomatopoeic rendering of the sound produced by the wooden beater or swizzle-stick used to raise a froth on the beverage. Others believe that *chocoatl*, which also meant "firewater," was a derivation of *xocoyac*, meaning "to ferment," or of *xococ* (sour, bitter). The question remains undecided to the present day.

Facing page: Easter eggs and fish. Chocolaterie Puyricard, Aix-en-Provence.

"So noble a confection is it, that chocolate, rather than nectar or ambrosia, is the true food of the gods."

Doctor Bachot, *An chocolatae usis salubris*, 1684.

FACTORIES

■ **FACTORIES**
The democratization of chocolate

Chocolate factories, the second strand of the chocolate industry after semi-prepared products (see Confectioners' coating), manufacture four types of product: molded* chocolate, including bars,* powdered* chocolate, chocolate spreads and chocolate confectionery* (chocolates* and confectionery bars).

The first chocolate factory set up in France,* the Compagnie Française des Chocolats et des Thés Pelletier & Compagnie, was opened in 1770. When the Menier* factory was established at Noisiel in 1824, it was equipped with steam-driven machinery: the age of chocolate for the masses had dawned. In 1828, a major discovery was made in the Netherlands* with Van Houten's perfection of the process of making cocoa powder.

Today, this sector of the industry is still occupied by some medium-sized businesses, such as Valrhona, an offshoot of the Chocolaterie du Vivarais, founded in 1922. But it is dominated by large European or international concerns, which in many cases themselves belong to major food conglomerates.

Industrialization ensured a basic minimum quality at a lower cost, and this in turn brought about the democratization of chocolate and a broadening of the potential market, which proved to be of equal benefit to master *chocolatiers.* The remarkable degree of creativity displayed by the latter, meanwhile, has proved an inspiration to the industry as a whole, threatened as it was by an increasing degree of uniformity. This symbiotic relationship is clearly evident in the field of flavor blending: the more inventive master *chocolatiers* exploit the technical advances achieved by the industry and the wealth of the cocoa *grands crus* (see Varieties) to develop new recipes, which in turn inspire the industrial giants; thus the chocolate bar containing slivers of cocoa beans,* developed by Michel Chaudun, is now marketed by Nestlé.

Fashion

In order to distinguish themselves from industrial manufacturers, some top-of-the-range chocolate producers and master *chocolatiers** have employed fashion designers to brush up their image. At the root of these partnerships there frequently lies a mutual passion for chocolate. Paco Rabanne was the first fashion designer to present a dress made of chocolate, at the second *Nuit du chocolat* in 1989. The idea of including a fashion show was taken up by the *Salon du chocolat*, organized in Paris every year by Sylvie Douce.

Fashion designer Sonia Rykiel, who melts with pleasure when confronted by the tiniest morsel of chocolate, created for Valrhona* its famous metal box inspired by a cigar box. She has also worked with Christian Constant and Michel Richart (see Design). Primrose Bordier chose vibrant colors to give a facelift to Weiss's chocolate boxes, and La Marquise de Sévigné appealed to Jean-Charles Castelbajac to banish the powdered marquesses from their boxes. The fashion house Moschino created a two-tone handbag featuring "dripping chocolate" in dark brown leather, which delighted its elegant Italian clientele (see Italy). From chocolate-shaped scented candles emanating warm, sweet scent, to perfumes by Thierry Mugler and Octée, the "drink of the gods" brings a note of fantasy, exoticism and elegance to this most ordinary of everyday treats.

Facing page: Stollwerk chocolate factory, Cologne, 1870.

Two-tone handbag by the fashion house Moschino. Private collection.

■ FRANCE

Hot chocolate* was introduced to the French court in the early seventeenth century by Queen Anne and Queen Maria Theresa, both of whom were of Spanish origin. After the invention of solid chocolate by the English in 1674, the French aristocracy also enjoyed it in the form of pastilles. Whatever form it took, French chocolate in the seventeenth and eighteenth centuries was frequently a mixture of cocoa and a range of flavorings: 'vanilla, cloves, cinnamon and sugar,' and also ambergris; Marie-Antoinette's personal *chocolatier* prepared her chocolate with 'powdered orchid, orange flower water or almond milk'.

The first chocolate factory in France was established in about 1687 in Bayonne.* The production of cocoa paste* was greatly simplified from 1732, the year in which du Buisson perfected a new system for grinding the beans,* using a tall horizontal table heated by means of a wood fire: the mechanization of chocolate manufacture (see Manufacturing process) had begun. But it was the Industrial Revolution of the nineteenth century which led to its complete democratization, thanks largely in France to the two great figures of Menier* and Poulain.*

Temporarily overshadowed by the rise of large-scale manufacturers, the master *chocolatiers** have acquired

a new and distinguished reputation in the last twenty years by turning more decisively towards a creative approach and the selection of *grands crus* (see Varieties), while retaining their centuries-old traditions. Marie-Antoinette's *pistoles* (chocolates* made with almond milk or orange flower water), still sold by Debauve et Gallais, the new ventures in aromas and design* by Michel Richart, the richly tempting ganaches* of Robert Linxe, the Japanese-inspired triumphs of Michel Chaudun, and Raymond Bonnat's French style *gianduja* (see Caffarel) are some of the many testimonies to the skills of French master *chocolatiers,* now recognized throughout the world.

Nonetheless, it is the chocolate bar* in block form which accounts for a large part (45 percent) of consumption in France today, closely followed by confectionery bars (35 percent), showing an increase of 180 percent in ten years: boxes of chocolates, meanwhile, remain a minority taste (17 percent). Dark chocolate,* with a high cocoa content (the French like it increasingly bitter) and sometimes mixed with hazelnuts or almonds, is also popular. Milk chocolate,* which is still the favorite, has now also started to boast of the pedigree of its *crus* (see Varieties).

Poster for Cémoi chocolate designed by Moupot, 1926.

Candied orange peel dipped in dark chocolate.

■ Fruit and nuts

The Swiss (see Switzerland) Charles-Amédée Kohler was the first to conceive of the idea of mixing hazelnuts with chocolate, in about 1830: crunchy, sweet and oily, hazelnuts provided a perfect contrast to the melting smoothness of milk chocolate* or the bitterness of dark chocolate.* Since that time, other dried fruits have been combined with chocolate bars,* most notably almonds and raisins. Hazelnuts and/or almonds are also found in high-quality praline* such as the great Italian speciality, the *gianduja* (see Caffarel).

As well as the classic hazelnuts, almonds (in the form of pieces or paste) and raisins (often soaked in rum), master *chocolatiers* also use pistachios and figs to create delicious fruit-and-nut combinations offering a sumptuous variety of textures and a kaleidoscope of flavors. Fine chocolate casings may be filled with walnuts and prunes ground to a paste. Strips of candied grapefruit or orange peel dipped in chocolate are also now a classic partnership; more acidic lemon makes another highly original but somewhat perilous association. The range of fruits preserved in spirits and encased in chocolate is ever-growing: apart from the traditional cherries in kirsch, *chocolatiers* now happily use raspberries and peaches.

Other specialties which make use of fruit include tablets of chocolate with hazelnut or almond pieces, whole cherries dipped in dark chocolate, and milk chocolate with raisins. Middle Eastern sweets often contain dates or orange flower water. Noteworthy iced desserts

(see Ices) include *Poire Belle-Hélène* with its mantle of hot chocolate sauce, and variations on the theme of the banana split. In *pâtisserie*,* chocolate is combined with apricot jelly in Sacher Torte and with Morello cherries in Black Forest gateau (see Austria and Germany).

It is possible to combine fresh fruit with chocolate, but unfortunately, the powerful aroma of cocoa and the natural acidity of fruit by no means bring out the best in each other.

■ Ganache

How many discoveries are the result of happy accidents? In the nineteenth century, the apprentice in a Paris *pâtisserie** spilt some scalding milk in a bowl of chocolate squares. In the face of this disaster, the patron called the lad a *ganache* (imbecile), but stirred the milk and chocolate together in the hope that the mixture might still be usable.

The end result, fluid and delicious, was to become the noblest base preparation in the master *chocolatier's* *repertoire: "of all the fillings available, ganache is certainly the finest as it contains the highest proportion of cocoa," declares the *chocolatier* Robert Linxe. Nowadays, the scalded cream is mixed with twice its weight in chocolate shavings; some cooks bind the mixture with butter to make it even more homogeneous. A perfect balance is thus achieved: the sugar neutralizes the acidity of the cream, and the rich smoothness of the cream mellows the bitterness of the cacao.

Flavoring the *crème fraiche* for a ganache requires experience, finesse and above all a touch of inspiration. The possible combinations seem almost infinite, indeed, and may include spices* and aromatics (cinnamon, cardamom, turmeric, cloves, mint, pepper, liquorice, saffron and vanilla), flowers (jasmine), fruit* (lemon, raspberry, mulberries and peaches), infusions (coffee,* tea and verbena) and spirits (see Alcoholic drinks).

Ganache is the main ingredient of truffles* and the filling for *palets d'or*, two great classics. The latter, created by

Bernard Serardy in 1898, consists of a coffee-flavored cream in a layer of fine chocolate sprinkled with flakes of gold— a veritable jewel for the tastebuds. *Palets d'or* are still made to this day, and the tradition has been taken up by every other master *chocolatier*. Some, such as Debauve et Gallais, make them using the principal cocoa *crus* (see Varieties).

Ganaches with tea. Mariage Frères, Paris.

The vogue for drinking chocolate, already established in Spain, reached the British Isles thanks to a Frenchman, who in 1657 opened the first chocolate factory in London. Unlike in France,* where it was a pleasure strictly limited to the aristocracy, this 'excellent West Indian drink' was made available to the middle classes from the outset. Soon, alongside the coffee* houses which made their appearance from 1652, there opened the first chocolate houses.*

London was also the setting, in 1674, for a historic invention: solid chocolate, presented in the form of 'Spanish rolls' or pastilles, and sold by the Coffee Mill and Tobacco Roll shop. Thus

attribution is disputed by the Italians), created by the Bristol firm of J.S. Fry and Sons in 1847.

But the symbolic father of British chocolate is undoubtedly John Cadbury (1801–1889). In 1824, Cadbury opened his first coffee, tea and chocolate shop. In 1831 he started manufacturing chocolate, and following his Quaker conscience and the example of the great French chocolate-manufacturer Menier* in caring for the social conditions of his workers, he created a model town for his employees in the Birmingham suburb of Bournville.

Eventually, Cadbury was to overtake the French firm and swallow up Poulain.* Today, Cadbury's is the largest manufacturer of confectionery* in Britain. Cadbury's Dairy Milk, created in 1905 and famously containing 'a glass and a half of full-cream milk,' and Bournville Plain drinking chocolate powder, created in 1907 from sweet dark chocolate,* are still very popular.

The British come sixth in the world league table of chocolate consumption,* eating their way through an average 7.6 kg per head of population annually. They are particularly fond of highly sweetened milk chocolate confectionery, consuming 70 percent of all confectionery bars sold in Europe.

Nowadays, Britain's most inventive master *chocolatiers*, some of them trained in France, create new recipes adapted to British tastes, using spices* such as cardamom or ginger and candied fruit*, such as the traditional rhubarb used in puddings.

it was that the British were to discover a taste for confectionery* which has never deserted them. The British were also responsible, in 1728, for the first factory equipped with hydraulic machinery, for the first clubs* exclusively for devotees of chocolate, and above all for the development of the chocolate bar* (although this

■ HEALTH
The virtues of indulgence

In the seventeenth and eighteenth centuries, chocolate was considered as much a medicine as a food, and numerous treatises* were devoted to its medicinal properties. In the nineteenth century, medicinal chocolates were put on sale, the flavor of the chocolate masking the sometimes unpleasant taste of the plants they contained.

Until the early twentieth century, chocolate was considered as a tonic (see Iron rations) when taken on an empty stomach, and as an aid to digestion when eaten at the end of a meal. It is therefore curious to note that, since the Second World War, chocolate has become the victim of widely accepted if unjustified suspicions of dubious origins (see Nutritional qualities).

Chocolate has been accused of causing migraines, acne and constipation, and although it has been completely

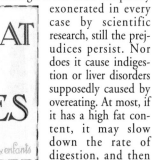

exonerated in every case by scientific research, still the prejudices persist. Nor does it cause indigestion or liver disorders supposedly caused by overeating. At most, if it has a high fat content, it may slow down the rate of digestion, and then only after a heavy meal. Allergic reactions to chocolate are moreover extemely rare. It is too often overlooked that dark chocolate,* which is particularly rich in cocoa, lowers cholesterol levels generally and slightly increases levels of benign HDL cholesterol, which helps to prevent fatty deposits on the arterial walls. Furthermore, the polyphenols contained in chocolate help to protect the body's blood vessels, and therefore contribute to the prevention of cardio-vascular disease as part of a healthy lifestyle.

Above:
Dummy display box for medicinal chocolate,
"*recommended for fragile stomachs and for convalescents and children.*"
Private collection.

■ Hershey's

Born in central Pennsylvania in 1857, Milton Hershey left school after the fourth grade and launched several smaller business ventures before finally creating the Hershey Chocolate Company which was to make both his fortune and his name. Founded in 1894, it is now the largest chocolate manufacturer in North America, as well as exporting to more than ninety countries worldwide. Among the many well-known brands in its range are Hershey's Kisses, Milk Duds, and Kit Kat as well as Cookies and Creme bars and Almond Joy.

Hershey's first company, set up in Lancaster, Philadelphia, specialized in caramels and made use of some of the very latest manufacturing equipment. However, in 1900 he sold this business for $1million, having decided to concentrate on making chocolate in the Pennsylvanian countryside, where he could easily get hold of the cheap, fresh milk he needed for his products. His mass-production techniques soon earned him the nickname of "the Henry Ford of chocolate" and he can justifiably be said to have revolutionized chocolate production in America. By 1905 the popularity of his products had earned Hershey enough to set up what has become the biggest chocolate factory in the world, near his home town of Derry Church. Like many other chocolate manufacturers, Hershey was a great philanthropist, setting up churches and parks for his workers. Nowadays Hershey's continues this tradition by running the Milton Hershey school and by sponsoring a Track and Field program for disadvantaged children.

■ Hot chocolate

In his *Historia del Mondo Nuovo* (1572), the botanist and explorer Girolamo Benzoni described how the Aztecs* prepared a drink made from cocoa: "They dry the beans* in an earthenware pot over a fire. Then they crush them between two stones to make a flour which they pour into goblets made from gourds. Then they mix them with water little by little and often put in some of their long pepper and drink it all." The beverage was then stirred with a beater, or *molinillo*, until the cocoa butter rose to the surface and could be skimmed off. The Aztecs flavored their chocolate with a considerable number of spices* and aromatics (ground chilli, aniseed, etc.) and sometimes colored it red with annatto (*Bixa orellana*), perhaps to give it the appearance of the blood drunk at human sacrifices.

Spanish colonists (see Spain) adapted the drink to their tastes by adding cane sugar. They prepared it with hot water (perhaps to dissolve the ingredients more easily?) and experimented with sweeter spices as flavorings: in 1630, the missionary

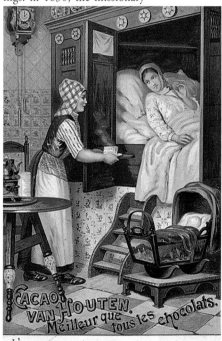

L'ALIMENT PRESCRIT PAR LE MEDECIN.
Une chambre à coucher à Hindelooper (Hollande)

Thomas Gage noted the use of cloves, cinnamon, almonds, vanilla, musk and ambergris.

In the seventeenth century, hot chocolate conquered Europe, with new variations in its preparation including the addition of a finger of wine or of

Above: "*The food prescribed by doctors.*" Advertisement for Van Houten cocoa powder. Private collection.

Luis Meléndez,
Still life (detail),
1776.
Museo del Prado,
Madrid.

most refined of palates. The first chocolate ice is mentioned at the Spanish court (see Spain) in the mid-seventeenth century, when the vogue for hot chocolate* was at its height. This consisted of a sorbet chilled in an "ice pit," as introduced during the reign of Charles V.

It was the invention of an ice cabinet, in about 1870, that made possible the development of new recipes. In profiteroles and *Poire Belle-Hélène*—named after the celebrated operetta of 1864—vanilla ice cream complements the flavor, while contrasting with a hot chocolate sauce. In 1922, the American Christian Nelson took the first vanilla ice cream on a stick and coated it with chocolate.

Devotees of milk chocolate* also tend to enjoy it in the form of unctuous ice cream, containing sugar, egg yolks, milk and full-fat cream to smooth the bitterness of the

milk,* a formulation which was to outstrip all others in popularity over the years.

For two centuries, Europeans prepared their chocolate using a sort of cocoa paste* solidified in the form of tablets or rolls and grated (Thomas Gage reported an identical practice among the Aztecs). The development of cocoa powder by Van Houten in 1828 was to make the preparation of hot chocolate considerably easier. Nowadays, the best cafés and tea rooms offer rich, smooth hot chocolate, made from pure cocoa powder or shavings. The preparation of these delicious drinks (see recipes inside the back cover) requires a little care and high-quality ingredients, but does not need any special utensils and so can easily be done at home.

Ices

In 1530, Marco Polo brought back the first recipe for ices from his travels in China. The Italians (see Italy) subsequently elaborated recipes to refresh the

Les Mangeurs de Glaces.

cocoa. In contrast, sorbets, the delight of dark chocolate* enthusiasts, contain no milk, cream or eggs: an excellent quality coating chocolate (see Confectioners' coating) and cocoa powder* are mixed with sugar syrup, and a turbine accomplishes the rest of the miracle.

■ Iron rations

Throughout military history, from the time of the Aztec warriors* to the marshals of the French Empire, the privates of the First World War and the troops of today, chocolate has always formed part of food rations. In order to remain alert on the battlefield, Napoleon I was said to drink numerous cups* of chocolate, served to him by his faithful majordomo Colin, who followed him everywhere. Following the French capture of Danzig in 1807, the emperor dubbed the victorious Marshal Lefebvre a duke and presented him with a box of chocolates. When Lefebvre opened the box that evening, he found that it contained banknotes to the value of three hundred thousand francs, a colossal sum. From then on, French soldiers habitually referred to their pay as *chocolat de Danzig*.

Napoleon III—no doubt recalling the battle of Solferino, during which his only sustenance was some chocolate he found in his saddlebag—declared on 5 January 1860: "Cocoa is not a luxury merchandise, nor is it an indulgence. Its hygienic and nutritive qualities are beyond dispute, and because it is endowed with an aroma and flavor which flatter the palate, it is among the goods of major consumption on which I proclaim a reduction in price. For it is physically and morally beneficial."

During the First World War, Banania drink*—a chocolate-flavored flour made from cocoa, sugar and banana flour which had just been discovered by Pierre-François Lardet, a pharmacist—was included in the rations of French troops in the trenches.

In the Second World War, chocolate bars (see Confectionery) were included in American G.I.s' basic rations. For units posted to the Pacific, the Pennsylvania Manufactory Confectioners' Association developed "Field ration D," a bar with added vitamin B1, which did not melt in temperatures of up to 100°F (38°C). Between 1941 and 1945, 500,000 of these bars were produced daily. This technological advance was to be pressed into service once more during both the Vietnam and Gulf Wars.

Facing page:
The Icecream Eaters. Lithograph by François-Séraphin Delpech after Louis Boilly, 1825. Bibliothèque nationale de France, Paris.

Advertisement for Whitman's Chocolate, *Life*, February 1943.

■ ITALY

The vogue for drinking chocolate was introduced to Italy in 1606 by Antonio Carletti, a Florentine merchant returning from Spain. The simplest of his recipes contained cocoa, sugar, vanilla and cinnamon. Members of the Italian aristocracy, however, like their French counterparts (see France), enjoyed experimenting with unusual flavorings, including citron and lemon, musk and ambergris and, at the court of the Medicis, jasmine. Antonio Ari was the first *cioccolatiere* to put the drink on sale in Turin, which by the seventeenth century had become the Italian chocolate capital, a distinction which it retains to this day. Eighteenth-century Turin saw the invention of chocolate *bavareisa*, or mousse, and above all of the delectable *bicerin*, a drink prepared with equal parts of coffee,* chocolate and cream, which

delighted Alexandre Dumas in 1852. The name is derived from the charming small glasses or *bicerin* in which it is still served today.

Turin was also the birthplace in 1861 of the *gianduja*, invented by Caffarel:* these ingot-shaped chocolates, with their meltingly smooth mixture of finely ground hazelnuts, walnuts and almonds, sugar and chocolate, are now famous throughout the world. The Italians are the greatest enthusiasts in Europe for bitter chocolate, often with a hazelnut or liqueur filling. But the most popular Italian chocolate worldwide is the small, praline-filled Ferrero *rocher*; with its cherry-filled Mon Chéri chocolates and Nutella spread, Ferrero alone accounts for 6 percent of the European market. The Bologna firm of Majani produces inimitable specialties such as the *cremino*, with layers of four different chocolates, created in 1911 to mark the launch of the Fiat Tipo 4. The traditional *tartuffo,* or truffle,* and hazelnut or cherry-filled *baci* (kisses), meanwhile, are sold at a daily rate of half a billion throughout the world. Finally, the small squares of chocolate known as neapolitans are now enjoyed with cups of coffee in virtually every country of Europe as well as in North America.

Box of *Baci* by Perugina,
designed by Federico Seneca, 1922.

Grangianduja
by Stratta, Turin.

LIQUEUR CHOCOLATES

Jean-Étienne Liotard, *La Belle Chocolatière*, 1745. Gemäldegalerie, Dresden.

■ Liqueur chocolates

The range of liqueur chocolates—whether liquid spirits in a chocolate case, or chocolates* filled with ganache* flavored with an alcoholic essence or extract—was developed in Europe in the 1920s. In their brightly colored foil wrappings, they liven up any chocolate box* assortment. Originally, the liquid was mixed with sugar syrup and poured into starch "pouches," which then crystallized into shells ready to be coated with chocolate. Indus-trial chocolate factories* still use essentially the same technique today. Master *chocolatiers* prefer to use ganache, the noblest of all chocolate base preparations because it has the highest cocoa content. Adding spirits to the point where only the very essence of the flavor lingers requires considerable finesse, in the ability to judge exactly the right amount required.

While the cherry-and-kirsch-filled varieties are among the most famous liqueur chocolates, the range of liqueurs and spirits used is in fact extensive. It includes whisky, cognac, armagnac and fine champagne; vintage rum, often combined with raisins in a bitter ganache; and liqueurs based on fruit,* such as kirsch, pear and plum brandy, and on plants, such as chartreuse.

Literature

No discussion of chocolate in literature would be complete without a mention of the Marquise de Sévigné (1626–1696), a dedicated follower of fashion who became a devotee of this exotic new drink, so highly regarded at court. The eight letters in which she discussed the subject, written between 1671 and 1675, indicate that her passion for chocolate ebbed and flowed as she came under the influence, in turn, of its admirers and detractors.

Among its most ardent admirers were Casanova and the Marquis de Sade, both of whom celebrated its aphrodisiac* qualities. Anthelme Brillat-Savarin* eulogized about it, while Honoré de Balzac was rather more sceptical in his *Traité des excitants modernes* (*Treatise on modern stimulants*): "Who can tell whether the abuse of chocolate did not play a part in the debasement of the Spanish nation, which, at the point when it discovered chocolate, was about to embark on the rebuilding of the Roman empire?"

Modern writers have also paid tribute to chocolate. Mexican author Laura Esquivel's novel *Like Water for Chocolate* tells

Lilian Harvey in the film *Du sollst nicht stehlen (Thou Shalt Not Steal)*, 1927.

of the thwarted love of a young couple and how their feelings for each other are sublimated through cookery, the title being a Latin American expression for seething passion. More recently still, the British author Joanne Harris entitled her best-selling novel simply *Chocolat*. The book, and film of the same name, recounts the tale of a mysterious *chocolatière* who settles in a small village and brightens the lives of the locals with her delicious chocolate creations. Enid Futterman's *Bittersweet Journey* is the tale of a heroine's quest for true love and chocolate.

In a more serious vein, the fine novels of Jorge Amado, such as *Cacao* (1994), describe the oppressive working conditions of the Brazilian cocoa plantations* at the beginning of the century: Amado himself was familiar with such hardships, being the son of a plantation owner. Chocolate is also a recurring subject in children's books, most famously in Roald Dahl's classics *Charlie and the Chocolate Factory* and *Charlie and the Great Glass Elevator*.

■ MANUFACTURING PROCESS: FIVE STEPS TO FINE CHOCOLATE

The first stage in the process of making chocolate involves mixing together in a kneading machine cocoa pastes,* sugar, vanilla and, in the case of milk chocolate,* milk powder. In order to obtain a smooth, granule-free mixture, the paste is then worked by multiple-roller refiners. This process reduces the cocoa and sugar particles to a size of less than thirty microns and ensures perfect blending of the dry and fatty components. This is followed by conching, an essential step which reduces any acridity and bitterness in the paste and also removes some of its last traces of humidity. The process was invented by the Swiss Rudolphe Lindt (see Switzerland), who patented it on 4 December 1880. Lindt's machine was called a *conche*, after its shell-like appearance (the Latin for shell is *concha*), and the name stuck. The process falls into two separate parts. First comes dry conching, in which friction

Unmolding and wrapping chocolate bars. Lindt-Sprüngli factory, Kilchberg, *c.*1880.

■ Market

The third most important agricultural product by volume on the international market, cocoa, like all basic commodities, is subject to the law of supply and demand.

The price of cocoa is quoted on the stock exchanges of Paris, New York and, above all, London. Major groups such as Cargill and E.D. & F. Mann are able to use their comprehensive knowledge of the production* of the various producer countries, in terms both of quality and of quantity, to predict world prices and speculate on harvests. The market has for many years been subject to sudden, repeated and very strong fluctuations, reflecting the tense relationship between the producer countries and countries which process the beans.* In West Africa, marketing boards guarantee a minimum price to plantation owners while between the cocoa particles and the sugar crystals is used to maximum effect to smooth their sharp corners. This is followed by wet conching, during which the cocoa butter* is added. Lastly, soya-derived lecithin, a natural emulsifier, may be added to render the mixture more liquid and homogeneous. During conching, the chocolate mass, kept at a temperature of 140–176°F (60–80°C), is mixed and smoothed for many hours. It is this process which gives chocolate its velvety-smooth texture, melting in the mouth.

After this comes tempering, in which the stable crystals of the cocoa butter are selected in order to obtain a homogeneous, glossy appearance and an even, non-granular texture, and to ensure good keeping qualities for the finished product (see Storage). After tempering, the chocolate is poured into metallic molds (see Molding) which are passed over vibrating tables in order to ensure that the paste is evenly spread and contains no air bubbles.

The molds then pass through cooling tunnels. The chocolate contracts as it crystallizes, finally slipping easily out of the molds. The chocolate is then ready to be wrapped.

Pre-grinding and grinding of chocolate, Barry Callebaut factory.

supervising negotiations for exporting the beans. The United Nations has tried in vain to stabilize the world cocoa market. Even in recent years, some countries have had to burn part of their harvest to avoid a collapse in prices. New European directives allowing vegetable fat to be used instead of a percentage of cocoa butter have also had a negative impact on the economies of producer countries.

Share certificate for Guérin-Boutron chocolate. Private collection.

MASTER CHOCOLATIER
Quality and creativity

In the majority of cases these days, chocolate is manufactured and marketed like any other product, but fortunately there still remain a few dedicated craftsmen who care enough about their work to produce chocolate of outstanding quality. Chocolate-making has acquired its professional credentials only in the last twenty years or so, owing largely to schools which set out to teach the arts of *pâtisserie* and the making of chocolate and confectionery. One of the most distinguished is the COBA in Basel (see Switzerland), whose alumni include some of the greatest master *chocolatiers* working today. *Chocolatiers* in France* derive their "recipe-based culture' from the training they share with *pâtissiers*, bakers and ice-cream makers. (It is regrettable, incidentally, that women make up only 10 percent of this trainee workforce, and that once qualified they are mostly accepted only for behind-the-counter work such as sales and packaging). Students are also given a basic grounding in biology, chemistry and mechanics, in order to enable them to master traditional manufacturing* techniques. After leaving college, they must then complete an apprenticeship of at least three years with a working *chocolatier*. Some may choose to become *compagnons*, or journeymen, combining the perfection of their skills with the notion of brotherhood through work in a system akin to the medieval guilds (see Masterpiece).

Currently, only very few *chocolatiers* make their chocolate starting from cocoa beans*. All the rest use chocolate bought from industrial suppliers (see Confectioners' coating), mixing them to produce their own distinctive product. Aiming at a discriminating market, they select their basic ingredients with scrupulous care, in the full knowledge that only by achieving a standard of excellence will they forge a reputation and gain a loyal clientele. Master *chocolatiers* are artists who have learned how to subdue the natural bitterness of cocoa; how to reveal the depth of its character through the secret alchemy of mixing varieties;* and finally how to reveal the full glory of chocolate by marrying it with other ingredients.

Masterpiece

Although we know chocolate can be molded,* it is often forgotten that it may also be sculpted. Indeed, its remarkable consistency lends itself to being worked with chisels, drills, and even hairdryers for the finishing touches. A variety of different-colored chocolates—dark,* russet or ivory lacquer—is used to give the initial block a marbled effect reminiscent of wood graining. Although a few distinguished artists such as César have tried their hand at chocolate sculpture, it is more generally practised by master *chocolatiers*,* who pit their skills against each other at professional competitions. Similarly, apprentice *chocolatiers* who have elected to travel round France as *compagnons*, or journeymen, are required to produce a sculpted "masterpiece" at the end of their training. The most remarkable pieces are frequently put on public display at chocolate trade fairs and international events:

Chocolate also lends itself to the making of models. The largest to date depicted the Olympic village in Barcelona: measuring some thirty feet (10 meters) in length and weighing no less than two tons, it earned itself a place in the *Guinness Book of Records*. Marcel Bonniaud is one of the many talented artists working in this field. Every year, he dresses his shop window in Lyons with detailed models of châteaux, cathedrals and other famous historic monuments—all carved out of chocolate.

Menier (Émile-Justin)

In 1825, Jean-Antoine Brutus Menier (1795–1853), a Paris pharmacist's assistant, bought a mill at Noisiel, in the Seine-et-Marne region, in order to grind his own medicinal powders. Later, he acquired a small neighboring chocolate factory,* since medicinal chocolates still formed part of the pharmacist's wares at that time. In 1853, the year of his death, the firm produced 200,000 tons of pharmaceutical products and a mere 3,000 tons of chocolate.

His son, Émile-Justin (1826–1881), took over the business, and steered it towards chocolate-making. Anxious to take charge of the whole chain of production, he bought cocoa plantations* in Nicaragua, chartered ships and acquired an interest in the sugar industry. Taking advantage of the development of advertising* which was just beginning to adopt aggressive marketing techniques, the firm was named "the world's most successful chocolate company" at the Universal Exhibition held in Chicago in 1893.

To woo his young customers, Émile-Justin Menier gave away ink blotters and exercise-book covers, and schools received free "educational boxes" containing a variety of different cocoa beans,* with which teachers might prepare lessons around the subject of chocolate.

Inspired by the ideas of Charles Fourier, Menier applied the principles of socialism to capitalist production, and at

Émile-Justin Menier.

This page: *The Aztec God Quetzalcoatl.* Chocolate sculpture by Michel Chaudun, 1996.

Facing page: Italian chocolate-maker's sign, late nineteenth century.

87

Above:
Menier factory,
Noisiel, c.1900.

Below:
Fondant au Lait
chocolate bar
wrapping.
Private collection.

Noisiel in 1874 he created a model town with gardens for his workers. They also benefited from free schools, libraries and medical care. Moreover, the grocer's shop sold products from the Menier farm at cost price, to be paid for in Menier tokens. Having entered the world of politics, Menier was elected to government in 1876.

Weakened by the 1929 depression and again by the Second World War, the factory finally shut in 1959. A masterpiece of ironwork and polychrome brick, renovated in 1860 and again in 1906 by Stephen Sauvestre (Eiffel's partner), it is now a classified monument, and since 1995 has been headquarters of Nestlé-France.

■ MILK
Condensed sweetness

Milk chocolate differs from dark chocolate* in containing a smaller percentage of cocoa solids (30 percent minimum), and in its additional sweetness and smoothness by virtue of its milk content (see Regulation). The recipe was perfected in Switzerland* by Daniel Peter in 1875. For many years, manufacturers had tried to find a way of mixing cocoa paste* with milk, in vain, due to

the latter's high liquid content. The invention of condensed milk by Henri Nestlé finally made this possible.

Milk chocolate, whether in the form of bars* or chocolates,* is now the most popular chocolate in the world, adapting itself to different national tastes: very sweet in the United States, toffee-flavored in Britain,*

milky in Switzerland and creamy in Belgium.* The most famous milk chocolate bar in Europe is Milka by Suchard,* created in 1901 and, since 1972, sporting a surrealist mauve cow against a background of Swiss alpine pastures. As consumers become more demanding, milk chocolate is increasingly made with good varieties* of cocoa. Its quality may be judged from its color, more or less ochre according to the volume of beans* included in its composition, and by its aroma of caramel, which should ideally be subtle and not too "toffeeish" so as not to overwhelm the flavor of the cocoa.

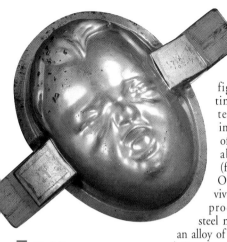

■ Molding

Christmas, Easter and even St Valentine's Day are now marked by shop displays featuring an impressive array of figures, Father Christmases, bells, eggs and chocolate hearts. And the chocolate money that children love to play with is a reminder that cocoa beans* were used as a form of currency by the Aztecs.*

Not until 1830, with the appearance of mechanical grinders which produced chocolate with a sufficiently fine texture, was it possible to carry out the first chocolate moldings. The great variety of subjects and shapes available nowadays is produced by melting coating chocolate (see Confectioners' coating) at 113°F (45°C), then cooling it to below its crystallization point, before finally raising the temperature again to 86°F (30°C).

Following this tempering process, the chocolate is poured onto the inner surface of the molds, also heated to 86°F (30°C), to a depth of quarter of an inch. After cooling, the final product is unmolded to reveal a glistening chocolate figure. Prominent tin mold manufacturers in France* included the firms of Pinat, Cadot and above all Letang (founded in 1832). Only the last survives today, faithfully producing stainless steel molds, made from an alloy of chrome and nickel. But these traditional molds are expensive, and can hardly compete with cheaper newcomers in thermo-plastic, silicone or Flexipan (glass with silicone).In Germany, the firm of Reiche (established in 1855) produces a catalog featuring 50,000 molds in platinol (nickel steel), a material that lends a glossy sheen to chocolate figures.

"Child's head" and "Father Christmas" chocolate molds. Private collection.

■ NETHERLANDS

Although the Dutch, together with the Flemish (see Belgium), were among the first people in Europe to sample the beverage prepared with grated cocoa, for many years they remained in ignorance of its recipe, which was jealously guarded by the Spanish (see Spain). According to the Dominican missionary Thomas Gage in the early seventeenth century, Dutch pirates who in 1585 ambushed a Spanish ship laden with cocoa beans* had no idea of the value of this precious cargo: they flung 'all this merchandise into the sea ... calling it, in bad Spanish, *cagaruta de carnero*' - that is, 'nanny-goats' droppings!' Nevertheless, before the century was out, ships of the Dutch East India Company were unloading their cargoes of cocoa beans on the quays of Amsterdam, transported from the Dutch colony of Surinam (ceded to them by the British in 1667). By the late eighteenth century, the former mustard mills along the River Zaam were being used to grind cocoa beans, in order to supply some thirty chocolate factories with their raw material.

But Holland's chief contribution to the art of chocolate-making undoubtedly came from Coenraad Johannes Van Houten, a chocolate-manufacturer in Amsterdam who invented cocoa powder* in 1815. Taking his inspiration from a technique described as early as 1679, he conceived a hydraulic press capable of extracting cocoa 'oil.' The dry residue from this process formed a 'cake' which needed only to be crushed and pulverized to produce a fine powder. Van Houten registered the patent in 1828, and went on to perfect what became known as the 'Dutching' process: alkaline salts were added to the paste* before pressing, making the powder less acid and easier to mix with water. The pungent dark-brown powder in its famous yellow Van Houten tin rapidly swept the market, bringing in its wake the democratization of hot chocolate,* hitherto the preserve of the wealthy few in Europe. Henceforth, Dutch manufacturers neglected eating chocolate in favour of cocoa

Above: Grinding cocoa.
Right: Advertisement for Van Houten cocoa powder, "*universally recognized as the best and cheapest of all chocolates.*"

Cacao van Houten
Universellement reconnu comme
Meilleur et moins cher
que tous les Chocolats.

powder. Since the nineteenth century, the largest names in the field have been Bensdorp, De Zaan, Gerkens and of course Van Houten.

Brought up on pure cocoa powder (without added sucrose or powdered milk), the Dutch favor quality over novelty or variety, preferring their chocolate dark* and bitter, as seen for example in the famous Droste pastilles.

Neuhaus (Jean)

Jean Neuhaus, from Neuchâtel in Switzerland,* went into partnership with his pharmacist brother-in-law in 1857 in order to open a shop selling medicinal confectionery in the most exclusive shopping arcade in Brussels.

On his partner's death, he asked his son Frédéric, then an apprentice confectioner, to take over the shop, and gradually pharmaceutical products gave way to chocolates.

From 1895, the running of this already flourishing family business fell to Frédéric's son, also called Jean like his grandfather. In 1912, the younger Jean ensured a place in history for the name of Neuhaus by inventing his "filling enveloped in chocolate": the celebrated praline chocolate. His wife Louise Agostini—the great-granddaughter of the sculptor of that name, from whom she clearly inherited her artistic talent—designed in 1915 the green and gold Napoleonic-style "N" which is still the firm's trademark. That same year, Jean registered the patent for a cardboard container for loose chocolates,* the famous *ballotin*, which enabled vendors to package praline chocolates without their being crushed, as had been the case with paper cornets.

Today, the firms of Neuhaus, Mondose and Jeff de Bruges (originally a French company) together form the Neuhaus-Mondose group.

Nutritional qualities

Chocolate is not merely an indulgence, it is also a nourishing food source (see Iron rations) which does not really merit its "wicked" reputation.

Martine and her problems

Chocolate: whim or necessity?

Often, Martine, you feel like eating a bar of chocolate... but you don't, because you think you shouldn't—and so you are being unfair to yourself.

You don't *want* chocolate: you *need* it! You've done the shopping and the housework, and still somehow found the energy to be the perfect hostess.

You are exhausted, your body urgently requires energy in compensation, and you naturally feel the urge to eat chocolate, because it is a balanced food which instanteously restores the essential elements that you have used up. You deserve it, so why feel guilty about tucking into a bar of chocolate!

"*Martine and her problems. Chocolate: whim or necessity?*" *Paris-Match* magazine, 1955.

A 4 oz (100 g) bar* contains 70 percent cocoa, 1/3 oz (9 g) protein, 1 1/4 oz (36 g) glucids (of which 30 percent is sugar), 1 1/2 oz (40 g) lipids (cocoa butter*) and 1/2 oz (14 g) fiber. It is therefore a potential source of vegetable protein and fiber. It also contains trace elements and minerals: dark chocolate* is rich in potassium (600 mg), magnesium (200 mg) and phosphorus (280 mg).

Many people hesitate to eat chocolate because they fear it

will make them put on weight, and certainly, with 520 kilocalories per 4-ounce (100 g) bar, it is not be recommended as part of a weight-loss diet. But a few chocolates* or squares of chocolate, or even a *pâtisserie** at the end of a meal, will not upset a balanced diet. Snacking between meals is much more likely to make you put on weight.

Milk chocolate* contains calcium but is less rich in cocoa, which is precisely the ingredient that is the most beneficial to health.* White "chocolate,"* on the other hand, which contains no cocoa mass (see Paste) but only cocoa butter and sugar (60 percent!), can hardly be called nutritious ...

Painting

In European painting, chocolate and its accessories—glasses, cups,* *chocolatières** and occasionally swizzle-sticks—occupy a prominent place in seventeenth- and eighteenth-century still lifes: some of the finest examples are those by Willem Claesz Heda, Francisco de Zurbarán, Antonio Pereda, Francois Desportes and Luis Meléndez (p. 78).

In the mid-eighteenth century, two images of chocolate—the wicked and the pure—coexisted side by side. In its saucier incarnation, the drink, endowed with aphrodisiac powers, lurks in an alcove behind a woman in a state of semi-undress (Noël Le Mire) or a beauty who has hastily thrown on a negligee (Pietro Longhi). Engravings depict tender *tête-à-têtes* or pairs of lovers drinking a reviving cup of chocolate (Johann Elias Rindinger, M. Engelbrecht). A more wholesome image of

chocolate is provided by works by François Boucher, William Hogarth and Pierre Le Mazurier, all of whom depicted family or drawing-room scenes in which adults and children gather round a tray of hot chocolate*. The maid carrying the chocolate sometimes became the sole subject of the painting, as in *La Belle Chocolatière* (p. 82) by Jean-Étienne Liotard.

In the twentieth century, Cappiello, Mucha, Moupot and Bouisset have all been

commissioned to design advertising* posters. Although he once claimed to be "mad about Lanvin chocolate", Salvador Dalí failed to find inspiration in this theme, unlike Marcel Duchamp, who included a chocolate grinder in two of his compositions, and Kurt Schwitters, who inserted a chocolate bar* wrapping in a Cubist collage. Certain contemporary artists have used chocolate as paint on their canvases, plain or dyed.

François Boucher,
Le Déjeuner,
1739.
Oil on canvas.
Musée du Louvre,
Paris.

■ PASTE
The art of blending

Coming after the initial treatment of the beans* in the producer* countries and before the fabrication of chocolate, the process of making cocoa paste involves cracking and winnowing, roasting, grinding, refining, conching and blending. It is usually carried out in specialist chocolate factories,* once small businesses, now major concerns.

Cocoa paste is produced from cocoa beans by means of a series of mechanical processes. After cleaning to remove any impurities, the beans are dried by a technique using infra-red light which facilitates the removal of the shells and the elimination of bacteria. Next, the cooled beans are coarsely crushed and the rough pieces, called "nibs," are roasted. The length and degree of roasting depend on the provenance of the varieties* and on the desired end-product, the purpose of this essential process being to develop the aromas formed during fermentation, to eliminate the last volatile acids, to lower the water content—from 8 percent to 2 percent—and to reduce the level of bacteria. There follows a milling process at 194°F (90°C), followed by refinement, to obtain a paste of fluid consistency, known as "cocoa paste," "mass" or "liquor", which still contains its original level of fat.

If cocoa powder* or butter* is desired, the paste is pressed in order to separate its oily content from the dry residue, known as "cake." Otherwise, it will continue the process of being turned into chocolate (see Manufacturing process).

The blending of various pastes, obtained from different varieties* of beans, determines the flavor and quality of the final chocolate. *Forastero* beans from Africa or Brazil predominate, with varying proportions of the finer *criollo* and *trinitario* varieties. Although chocolate of "pure origin" (made from beans of a single provenance) has its fans, the end product, like wine, is usually the result of subtle blending.

Pâtisserie

Originally a rare and costly commodity, chocolate entered the world of *pâtisserie* by stealth in the seventeenth century, as a flavoring. The earliest recipe to be based on chocolate was Sacher Torte, devised in Austria* in 1778. Only since the nineteenth century has chocolate become an ingredient in cakes, and now there are countless variations on the theme of chocolate cake worldwide.

Across Europe,* local *pâtisseries* offer chocolate eclairs to entice children, chocolate cream buns to seduce adults, and chocolate macaroons for grandmother's tea. Chocolate desserts, creams, mousses and charlottes are easy to make and remain firm fami-

ly favorites, while the chocolate log remains a great classic. German Black Forest gateau, meanwhile, conquered Europe years ago. Creative *chocolatiers* have introduced ganache* as an ingredient in a number of desserts, including chocolate tart with its irresistible contrast between the crisp sweetness of the pastry crust and the velvety bitterness of the cream filling. The internationally renowned *pâtissier* Gaston Lenôtre has rejuvenated old recipes by reducing their fat content, while other masters such as Philippe Conticini, Pierre Hermé and Yannick Lefort are now leading exponents of creative chocolate pastries and desserts.

Facing page, from top to bottom: pre-drying of beans under infra-red light; roasting; refinement; "cake." Barry Callebaut factory.

Below:
A selection of fine chocolate cakes, including the celebrated Austrian Sacher Torte (center right), along with chocolate macaroons, tarts and muffins.

■ PLANTATION
Around the world in four hundred years

Having grasped the potential interest of Aztec* cultivation*
of the cacao tree,* the Spanish (see Spain) created great plantations in central America in the sixteenth century. In the
seventeenth century, the British succeeded in acclimatizing
the tree in Jamaica, as did the French in Martinique and the
Dutch in Surinam. In the eighteenth century, cacao cultivation reached Brazil, where the plantations rapidly flourished.
Not until 1822 did the cacao tree cross the Atlantic, initially
reaching the island of São Tomé, in those days a Portuguese
colony. Plantations subsequently spread at a tremendous rate
across continental Africa, reaching Ghana (then the Gold
Coast) in 1879, before spreading to Nigeria, to the Ivory
Coast in 1905, and finally to Cameroon. At the end of the
nineteenth century, the Dutch introduced the cacao tree to

Java and Sumatra. The New Hebrides, New Guinea and Samoa joined the ranks of the producer nations* in the early twentieth century. All in all, it had taken the cacao tree four hundred years to travel round the globe. Furthermore, everywhere the cacao tree went, the coffee shrub followed (though the reverse was not the case, as coffee plantations cover a much greater geographical area in Africa).

Delicate and difficult to cultivate, the cacao tree knows no dormant season: it requires careful tending throughout the year, with regular harvesting of the pods. Little has changed in techniques of cultivation over the centuries. The novelist Jorge Amado, the son of a plantation owner, has described the harsh life of the Brazilian plantations and the conditions endured by workers, themselves the descendants of slaves (see Literature).

Beans drying on the roofs of a plantation, Trinidad.

Poulain (Victor-Auguste)

Victor-Auguste Poulain (1825–1918) was born near Pontlevoy, in the Loir-et-Cher region of France, and at the age of nine left home to work in grocers' shops. At the age of thirteen, he went to Paris to complete his apprenticeship at the *Mortier d'Argent*, a delicatessen frequented by the writer Honoré de Balzac, which manufactured its own delicious chocolate.

In 1847, Poulain took his savings and moved to the town of Blois, married, and started making and selling chocolate. His policy of offering a quality product at a low price brought customers flocking, and he was obliged to enlarge his premises on several occasions.

In 1862, he bought a piece of land and built a factory,* which he stocked with the latest machinery, updated as new developments improved equipment.

Famous for the quality of his chocolate, Poulain found himself the victim of imitation and forgery, which prompted him to launch his famous slogan, "*Goûtez et comparez*" ("taste and compare"). To strengthen his firm's image he entered competitions, winning numerous medals which were displayed prominently on the wrappings of his chocolate bars.* An innovator in the field of advertising,* he attracted children by adding metal figures or colored lithographs—

Poulain soluble chocolate powder tin. Private collection.

now collector's items (see Collecting)—to his tins of chocolate. He retired from business in 1878 and died on 30 July 1918, devastated by the fire which had destroyed his factory three weeks earlier. The chocolate-making business, which had become a limited company in 1893, is now part of the Cadbury-Schweppes group.

Powder

Who does not have distant memories of chocolate powder being spooned into a big cup, followed by sugar and a slow trickle of steaming-hot milk,* and of the pleasure of stirring the thick, frothy mixture?

It is to the Dutchman Coenraad Van Houten (see Netherlands) that we owe the invention, in 1828, of a pure but easily soluble cocoa powder. "Chocolate powder," on the other hand, is required to have a minimum cocoa content of only 32 percent, mixed with sugar. In France,* Poulain* popularized this type of product with the launch, in 1904, of his famous orange tin of chocolate powder; today, Poulain Grand Arôme is the second largest selling brand in France.

Preparations including ingredients other than cocoa and sugar may only call themselves "breakfast" chocolate. An example is Nesquik by Nestlé, flavored with cinnamon, and aptly named as it dissolves instantly. Launched originally in the United States, it is now

Advertisement for
Kwatta soluble
cocoa.
Private collection.

the most widely sold chocolate
drink in the world.

Different countries have
different drinking habits: in
France, 83 percent of house-
holds with children remain
faithful to their morning cup of
hot chocolate* (though this
pre-eminence is now threatened by the rise of breakfast
cereals). The Spanish drink it
at tea-time or in the evening:
the British drink it just before
they go to bed. The Americans
drink it at any time of day. The
Dutch, meanwhile, boast the
production of the finest-quality
cocoa powder, which they prefer with no sugar added.

Facing page:
Conquistador,
chocolate praline
by Bernard
Dufoux
containing
almonds,
pistachios,
hazelnuts and
candied orange.

Advertisement for
Van Houten
cocoa.
Private collection.

■ Praline

Invented in the early seventeenth century by the Maréchal
de Plessis-Praslin, Duke of
Choiseul, praline is "a mixture
composed of caramelized sugar,
almonds or hazelnuts, roasted
or not, with a minimum proportion of 50 percent nuts."
The toffee with the nuts mixed
in it is cooled in sheets before
being crushed between mill-
stones made of granite (which
leaves no taste). The resulting
mixture should contain slivers
of almond or hazelnut which
are large enough to be dis-
cernible on the palate yet fine
enough to allow a harmonious
blending of flavors and a sufficiently smooth texture. The
sugar should not be too obvi-
ous, to avoid the risk of over-
powering the delicate
personality and flavor of the
nuts.

When mixed with cocoa paste,*
praline becomes chocolate praline, used most commonly as a
filling for chocolates* or chocolate bars.* The quality of the
nuts is of fundamental importance. The best almonds come
from Provence, Italy,* or
Greece, while the finest hazelnuts come from Piedmont,
which explains the creation in
Italy of the *gianduja,* an ingot-
shaped chocolate filled with
praline containing between 20
and 40 percent hazelnuts.

■ Producer nations

For the countries that produce
cocoa beans,* many of which
belong to the Third World (see
Plantation), the cultivation* of
the cacao tree* and the industries that depend on it (fabrication of cocoa paste,* butter and
powder*) are essential sources
of income and employment. In
1900, world production of

Woman mixing cacao seeds, island of São Tomé.

105,000 tons was divided between Latin America (80 percent, led by Ecuador), Africa (15 percent) and Asia (5 percent). Today it has reached a figure of 2,700,000 tons, and its geographical distribution has been reversed in favor of Africa (65 percent in 1996), followed by Latin America (18 percent) and Asia and Oceania (17 percent).

The biggest world producer by far is the Ivory Coast (40 percent), followed by Ghana (13 percent) and Indonesia (11 percent). In a few years, Indonesia succeeded in overtaking Brazil's production rates by selling medium-quality beans at a price 30 or 40 percent lower than African varieties.* For the Ivory Coast, already suffering from the over-production weighing heavily on the world market,* and dependent on the European Union to take 70 percent of its exports, the consequences of a new European regulation* authorizing the use of vegetable fat in chocolate, hence reducing the demand for cocoa butter, are a matter of considerable anxiety, as the country's income is likely to plummet as a result. Since the beginning of the century, several generations of its people have owed their schooling to income from the cocoa industry.

Quetzalcoatl

Quetzalcoatl, priest-king of the Toltecs, held sway in the tenth century from his capital city, Tula, a place of legendary plenty, beauty and luxury. He was venerated as a god because he had given the cacao tree* to men, and had shown them how to cultivate it. But, filled with overweening pride, he dared to aspire to immortality, seeking out the sorcerer Tezcatlipoca to this end. Jealous of Quetzalcoatl, Tezcatlipoca gave him a potion which drove him mad. Fleeing to the riverbank, he took to the water on a raft made of serpents intertwined. As he drifted off towards the east he prophesied: "I shall return in a year of the reed, when I shall reclaim my power. This will be a time of great suffering and hardship for my people."

The centuries passed, but the Aztecs* did not forget the gardener-god responsible for the gift of the cacao tree, worshipping him under the name of "Votan", meaning "winged serpent". In 1519, a year of the reed, omens foretold grave events in store. A comet appeared in the sky, and an earthquake shook the land. Wise men and astrologers predicted that Quetzalcoatl would return on 21 April of that year. When, by an extraordinary coincidence, Cortés* landed on the coast on that very day, the Aztec king, Montezuma, was convinced that the "winged serpent" had indeed come back. With this tragic misconception, the Spanish conquest of the Aztecs was sealed. By the time they realized their mistake it was too late, and their attempts at resistance were futile; they were to endure great suffering and hardship until their civilization was obliterated.

Quetzalcoatl. Illustration from the *Codex Magliabechiano*, 1566. Biblioteca Nazionale Centrale, Florence.

Regulation

In the eighteenth and nineteenth centuries, chocolate was a luxury commodity. In order to undercut the competition, unscrupulous chocolate-makers sold adulterated products containing a surprising variety of substitutes for cocoa and cocoa butter.* Legislation against such fraudulent practices was gradually introduced in the first half of the century.

Since 1973, chocolate confectionery,* bars,* powders* and spreads have all been subject to a European directive on cocoa and chocolate, defining standards for designation, norms, composition and labelling. This states that dark chocolate* should contain at least 43 percent cocoa paste,* over 26 percent cocoa butter* and less than 57 percent sugar, with the cocoa content given on the packaging; milk chocolate* should contain a total of 30 percent dry cocoa solids, 18 percent dried milk solids, 26 percent total fat and at least 4.5 percent butter fat. In the United States, dark chocolate must contain a minimum of 35 percent cocoa paste, milk chocolate at least 10 percent.

In 2000, a new European directive provided controversy in Europe, favoring certain industrial chocolate-making concerns in the member countries, who, seeking to lower their production costs, had asked the European Union to authorize the replacement of 5 percent of the cocoa butter by vegetable fat—a request that was accepted. Master *chocolatiers** all over Europe opposed this move, but their struggle was fruitless and the suggestion has been adopted. Many chocolate lovers consider that this ruling has given rise to the production of ersatz chocolate that is not worthy of the name.

The Spanish receiving gifts of cocoa beans. Engraving from *The History of America* by Jean-Théodore de Bry, Frankfurt, 1600.

SPAIN: THE CONQUEST OF COCOA

After sailing from Cadiz on his fourth and last voyage to the New World, Christopher Columbus (1451–1506) landed on

the Caribbean island of Guanaja on 30 July 1502. He wrote in the ship's log: "A large native boat with twenty-five oarsmen came to meet us, their chief presented us with fabrics, fine copper objects and almonds which they use as money and with which they prepare a drink." The West had encountered cocoa beans before,* but the Genoese explorer had little conception of the importance of the gift he had received. He brought the beans back to Ferdinand II of Aragon, who had financed his expedition, and there the matter rested.

■ Spice

The original chocolate, as drunk by the Aztecs,* was flavored with pungent spices. Europeans sweetened the recipe but also experimented with a great variety of aromatic associations. As the years went by, chocolate became more subdued, reserving its favors for cinnamon and vanilla. These once exotic commodities are

Vanilla pods, cinnamon sticks and dark chocolate.

The discovery of chocolate would have to wait for the conquest of the Aztec empire by the Spanish conquistador Cortés,* nearly two decades later.

The Spanish colonists who arrived in the New World were far from convinced by the Aztec habit of drinking chocolate; indeed Girolamo Benzoni declared: "This mixture is more like pigswill than a drink for human consumption." But when they had used up their wine stores and grown bored of water, they sought ways of improving the Aztec recipe for chocolate. Some nuns from Oaxaca had the idea of sweetening it with cane sugar, vanilla and orange-flower water. Now even Benzoni had to admit that chocolate had become more than acceptable: "It is bitter in taste, but it quenches the thirst and refreshes the body."

Although Cortés brought the first cargo of beans back to Spain in 1528, the first business making chocolate, supplied by regular imports of beans, was not established until 1580. In the nineteenth century, Brillat-Savarin* noted that it was still true that "throughout the Peninsula, chocolate is presented at every occasion upon which etiquette demands the serving of refreshments." The Spanish passion for chocolate has since waned considerably, and they are now among the smallest consumers in Europe (see Consumption).

now frequently used to flavor ganache,* alongside the rarer ginger.

In their quest for the essential flavor of the bean,* master *chocolatiers* have recourse to a daring range of spices, savory as well as sweet. Michel Chaudun uses pepper and green cardamom, Robert Linxe fennel, and Michel Richart curry, to create startling but unforgettably rich fusions. Bernard Dufoux produces a range of chocolates using fresh plants each season, and Joël Durand has made inspired use of lavender. Working with spices and aromatics requires creative inspiration and subtle judgement, the cream to be used in ganache being infused with their aromas before it is mixed with the chocolate. Finally, in certain Latin American countries, and also in Italy* and Spain,* chocolate is used as a spice in cooking.

■ STORAGE: EAT IT QUICKLY!

Solid chocolate has a few enemies, which may appear during storage. Refrigeration does it no good at all: after hardening the inside, the cold produces a layer of condensation which

destroys its glossiness and gives it a whitish appearance, and which most importantly "kills" its flavor. Nor does chocolate enjoy the heat. At temperatures of above 82°F (28°C), its surface melts, and as it cools the cocoa butter* crystallizes to give it a whitish appearance. Although it is perfectly safe to eat in this state, some of the pleasure is undoubtedly lost. The ideal temperature for chocolate is between 59 and 64°F (15–18°C). Light can also cause the cocoa butter to break down and lose some of its palatability. It is therefore advisable to store chocolate in a dry place and inside a sealed box or tin, to protect it from surrounding odors which, like any substance with a high fat content, it will absorb to the detriment of its own flavor. For the same reason, chocolate bars* should be stored in their wrappings. Finally, the only sure way of avoiding all these dangers—especially if the chocolate is filled with a cream or butter ganache*—is to eat it as quickly as possible.

Advertisement for
Suchard chocolate
and cocoa, 1890.
Private collection.

Advertisement for
Suchard Milka
chocolate.
Private collection.

Suchard (Philippe)

Philippe Suchard (1797–1884) began his apprenticeship with his confectioner brother in Berne. After spending a year in the United States, he returned to Switzerland* and became a confectioner in Neuchâtel in 1825. The following year, he set up a factory at Serrières, powered by a paddle wheel, where he succeeded in producing 66 pounds (30 kg) of chocolate daily with only one employee. By the late 1840s, he was producing four sorts of chocolate bar* and pastilles called *diablotins*. As the business grew, so did Suchard's reputation. His chocolate was awarded gold medals at the Great Exhibition in London in 1851, and at its Paris counterpart in 1855. From 1880, Suchard opened branches in Germany (see Austria and Germany) and France,* followed by other European countries and the United States.

The famous Milka bar was launched in 1901, with the image of a St Bernard dog. This gave way in 1972 to the famous mauve cow, still in place today. After numerous mergers, the business is now part of the large Kraft-Jacobs-Suchard group.

■ SWITZERLAND

Switzerland was a latecomer in the discovery of chocolate, which came with its growth in economic prosperity in the eighteenth century. In 1750, Italian *cioccolatieri* sold rolls of cocoa paste* in Swiss markets, but not until 1792 was the first Swiss confectionery and chocolate business established, in Berne. Yet this small country was to produce not only important technical advances but also three major new recipes: chocolate with hazelnuts, milk chocolate* and fondant chocolate.

François-Louis Cailler (1796–1852), who had learned the art of chocolate-making in Italy* and founded a factory near Vervey in 1819, perfected the grinding process with the use of a machine worked by hydraulic power. His success proved an inspiration to others, such as Charles-Amedée Kohler (1790–1874), who started his career in chocolate in 1830, and in order to stand apart from the competition mixed hazelnuts with chocolate for the first time.

In 1875, Daniel Peter (1836–1919), son-in-law of François-Louis Cailler, adapted the process for condensing milk discovered by the chemist Henri Nestlé (1814–1890): thus milk chocolate was born, earning worldwide fame for Switzerland. Soon, the Société Suisse de Chocolats, founded in 1904, was to unite the four great names of Cailler, Kohler, Peter and Nestlé.

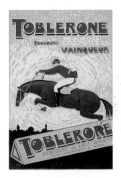

Advertisement for Toblerone,
by Jean Tobler.

But Switzerland's most remarkable commercial success must be Philippe Suchard's* Milka bar, launched in 1901 and still for many the chief symbol of Swiss chocolate; Suchard remains the best-known brand of Swiss chocolate in Europe.

Another great figure, Rudolphe Lindt (1823–1893), was the father of fondant chocolate. To achieve this level of creamy smoothness, in 1879 he perfected a new refining process, to become known as 'conching' (see Manufacturing process), and he increased the amount of cocoa butter* in his paste.* David Sprüngli bought up both the business and the miraculous recipe in 1899.

The Swiss are particularly fond of milk chocolate, chocolate with hazelnuts and also white chocolate,* and in general prefer their chocolate milky and rather sweet.

Tax

In 1659, Louis XIII granted letters patent for the sole rights to the sale of chocolate in France* to David Chaillou. In 1692, Louis XIV introduced a tax on cocoa to help finance France's war effort; and seven years later, the right to market drinking chocolate was sold to one hundred and fifty lemonade merchants, thus swelling the state's coffers once more. In 1704, Frederick the Great imposed a tax on chocolate in Prussia in an attempt to reduce foreign imports. Anyone wishing to nibble on some chocolate had to pay two thalers for the privilege.

In 1860, Napoleon III lifted the tax on chocolate in France as part of his drive to promote the drink and thus reduce alcoholism among the working classes. A similar effect was seen in Great Britain when Prime Minister Gladstone lowered the chocolate tax in 1853. Prices fell, and the chocolate industry boomed as a result. Unscrupulous manufacturers began to adulterate their product with cheaper alternative ingredients, leading ultimately to a series of regulations about what true chocolate may contain, which are in vigor to the present day.

Nowadays, the French chocolate industry is subject to an odd VAT ruling. Bars* of dark chocolate,* cocoa butter,* *pâtisserie** and biscuits, powders and flours, desserts and puddings are subject to a flat rate of 5.5 percent (the same rate as all food products in France). By contrast, all chocolate sold other than in bar form—such as flakes, granules, pastilles or individual chocolates,* for instance—is subject to a rate four times higher!

Title page from *Le bon usage du thé, du caffé et du chocolat* by Nicolas de Blegny, 1687.

Treatise

The first works to make reference to chocolate were written by the commentators who accompanied the Spanish conquistadors (see Spain). Some of these were genuinely ethnological in their approach: in his

Historia del Mondo Nuovo (1572), for instance, Girolamo Benzoni described how the Aztecs* prepared their drinking chocolate, and how the Spanish gradually came to accept it and then developed a passion for it. On its arrival in Spain and later in France,* chocolate was at first considered a remedy. Thus in 1643, at the command of Cardinal de Richelieu, Doctor René Moreau penned a curious four-part dissertation entitled *Du chocolat*, in which he discussed the drink's effect on health* and its modes of preparation. Also at this time, men of the church* such as Léon Pinelo were engaged in an exchange of abuse and diatribes on the thorny question of whether or not drinking chocolate broke the fast. Numerous seventeenth-century treatises evoked the virtues of coffee, tea and chocolate, notably Philippe-Sylvestre Dufour's *Traités nouveaux et curieux du café, du thé et du chocolat* of 1671, and Nicolas de Blegny's *Le bon usage du thé, du caffé et du chocolat* of 1687. Once the religious and medical arguments had died down, chocolate made its appearance in cookery books: the first to make reference to it, in recipes for biscuits and savory dishes, was by Massialot in 1692. Finally, it became the subject of encyclopaedia entries, as in Diderot and d'Alembert's famous *Encyclopédie* of 1752.

■ Truffle

From a symbolic point of view, it is interesting to note that the truffle, the "black diamond" of the gastronomic world, has its *alter ego* in the sophisticated world of chocolate. And while

Chocolate truffles by Robert Linxe.

the botanical variety grows in secret among the roots of oak trees, its frivolous cousin is to be found more often in the shade of a Christmas tree. Chocolate truffles—minor miracles of shameless indulgence—consist of a cream or butter ganache* roughly shaped into small balls. A dark chocolate* coating protects them from the effects of damp and the atmosphere, followed by a dusting of cocoa powder. Industrial manufacturers (see Factory) use vegetable fat to produce truffles with a longer shelf-life (see Storage). *Chocolatier* Henri Le Roux has created a "truffle-flavored truffle," a unique combination of ganache and fresh truffle. In this breathtaking partnership, the latter imparts its generous aroma to the former, making it linger even longer on the palate.

Harvesting cocoa pods, Cameroon.

■ VARIETIES: THE THREE "GIANTS"

Each of the three botanical varieties of cacao tree—the *criollo*, the *forastero* and the *trinitario*—yields specific varieties of bean* according to the nature of the land on which it is cultivated (see Plantation).

The *criollo* ("creole" in Spanish) is the original cacao tree of the Mayan civilization in Mexico, delicate and hence rare: it accounts for less than 5 percent of world production.* Highly perfumed, subtle and aromatic in flavor, it varies greatly in different regions of production. The most famous *crus* include Chuao, Puerto Cabello and Porcelana from Venezuela, Sambirano

from Madagascar and the Indonesian *criollo*. They are seldom used in pure form, and even in small quantities will enhance the quality of a mixed blend.

The *forastero* ("foreigner" in Spanish) originates from the high Amazon. Dubbed the "robusta of cocoa" because of its toughness and its high levels of tannin, this is the predominant variety in Africa and throughout the world (85 percent). Although African varieties are fairly ordinary, and are used essentially in industrial manufacture or as the basis of blends, there are also more distinguished *crus*, such as Arriba (or Nacional) from Ecuador and Trinidad, and Maragnan from Brazil and Venezuela.

The *trinitario*, lastly, is a hybrid of the *criollo*, from which it takes its elegant aroma, and the *forastero*, from which it derives its robust constitution. First cultivated in Trinidad, it is now also cultivated in Latin America, Sri Lanka and Indonesia, and accounts for between 10 and 15 percent of world production. The finest *crus* come from Trinidad (Santa Severa) and Java, and its lingering, fruity flavor has earned it the nickname "the Medoc of cocoa", named after the famous French wine. Research is today continuing to develop new high-quality hybrids on robust stock.

Versailles

Drinking chocolate appeared at the French court (see France) with Anne of Austria, daughter of Philip III of Spain,* who married Louis XIII in 1615. In 1660, their son Louis XIV married another Spanish princess, Maria Theresa, who was equally fond of the beverage. But it was the royal favorites who brought it definitively into vogue. Madame de Maintenon, to whom Louis XIV never refused anything, persuaded him to serve chocolate at court on feast days, and during his reign (1643–1715), Versailles imposed its taste for the beverage on high society as a whole. Ninon de Lenclos offered it to all the aristocrats of her acquaintance, and even introduced Voltaire to it. From the end of the seventeenth century, it was considered good form always to carry a small supply of chocolate pastilles, kept in exquisite little *bonbonnières*. Madame de Pompadour, a firm believer in the aphrodisiac*

Nicolas Bonnart, *A gentleman and his lady drinking chocolate*, late seventeenth century. Engraving. Bibliothèque nationale de France, Paris.

113

WHITE CHOCOLATE

properties of chocolate, had it served to her at dinner, flavored with vanilla and ambergris and accompanied by celery soup and a handful of truffles—an odd combination! Her successor in Louis XV's affections, the hot-blooded, young and beautiful Comtesse du Barry, was an equally passionate devotee of chocolate.

Marie-Antoinette created the post of "chocolate-maker to the queen", which she bestowed first on the Chevalier de Saint-Louis and afterwards on the famous *chocolatier* Debauve.

Madame du Barry. Engraving after Jacques-Fabien Gautier-Dagoty (1710–1781).

■ White chocolate

Can white chocolate really claim to be chocolate? While the regulations require chocolate to contain at least 25 percent cocoa, white chocolate contains at least 20 percent cocoa butter.* Its other ingredients, by law, are 14 percent dried milk products and 55 percent sugar. Its color makes it useful for decorating Easter* eggs and chocolate Father Christmases, and some professionals use it as a fixative for food colorings. In Belgium,* the celebrated Manon is often encased in white chocolate to create an initial melting sensation in the mouth. For those with a sweet tooth, Switzerland* produces it in bar* form.

Dark chocolate, milk chocolate and white chocolate.

c. 400 Probable date of first cultivation of the cacao tree, by the Mayan civilization in Yucatán.

c. 500 The existence of a cocoa-based drink is attested by traces in a pot found during archeological excavations in Guatemala.

c. 900 Quetzalcoatl reigns over the Toltecs. He is subsequenly deified, to be worshipped by the Aztecs as the god of chocolate.

1502 Christopher Columbus arrives on the island of Guanaja and receives a gift of cocoa beans.

1519 Hernán Cortés lands on the coast of present-day Mexico and embarks on the conquest of the Aztec empire. The conquistadors encounter the drink of chocolate.

1528 Cortés brings back to Charles V some cocoa beans and utensils for making chocolate.

1569 Controversy starts within the church as to whether or not liquid chocolate breaks the fast.

1580 Cocoa beans start arriving regularly in Spain, and the first workshops for making chocolate are established. Flanders (present-day Belgium and the Netherlands), then under Spanish dominion, discovers chocolate.

1591 Juan de Cardenas writes the first medical work dealing with the effects of chocolate on health.

1606 The merchant Antonio Carletti, returning from Spain, introduces the vogue for drinking chocolate to Italy.

1615 Louis XIII marries Anne of Austria, daughter of Philip III of Spain; fond of chocolate, she introduces it to the French court.

1640 Chocolate arrives in Austria via Italy. Monastic communities spread its use through the Holy Roman Empire.

1650 The first cacao plantations in the West Indies. Towards the middle of the century, drinking chocolate starts to be prepared with milk.

1657 The first British factory making chocolate is set up in London.

1660 Louis XIV's marriage to Maria-Theresa of Austria, daughter of Philip IV, encourages the court's taste for chocolate.

1674 The London shop Coffee Mill and Tobacco Roll offers solid eating chocolate for the first time, chiefly in the form of pastilles.

1679 The first West Indian beans arrive in Brest.

1681 The French revenue appropriates the monopoly on the cocoa trade.

1692 Louis XIV institutes a tax on cocoa to help finance his war effort.

1725 Louis XV marries Marie Leszcynka. Although not Spanish, she is a chocolate enthusiast, as are the royal favorites, who prize its virtues as an aphrodisiac.

1727 A cyclone devastates the cacao plantations in the French West Indies.

1732 Du Buisson invents a tall horizontal table for grinding cocoa, which improves working conditions in chocolate factories.

1740 Chocolate remains a costly commodity; unscrupulous manufacturers attempt to increase their profits by selling adulterated chocolate.

1750 Switzerland discovers chocolate thanks to Italian chocolate-makers selling their wares in Swiss markets.

1765 Chocolate is first manufactured in the United States by John Hanan and James Baker at Milton Lower Mills, near Dorchester, Massachusets.

1770 Pelletier opens the first 'industrial' chocolate factory in France: the *Compagnie française des Chocolats et des Thés.*

1776 The first advertisement for chocolate, by Sieur Roussel, appears in *Le Mercure de France.*

1778 Doret invents a hydraulic machine for grinding cocoa paste and mixing it with sugar. The first chocolate-based *pâtisserie*, Sacher Torte, is created in Austria.

1780 Debauve is appointed *chocolatier* to the French queen.

1804 In his *Almanach gourmand*, Grimod de la Reynières mentions four Parisian *chocolatiers* worthy of praise, including Debauve.

1807-8 The Contintental blockade disrupts imports of cocoa and sugar. Cocoa becomes prohibitively expensive and adulterated chocolate proliferates.

1815 The Van Houten chocolate factory is founded in the Netherlands.

1819 Pelletier equips his factory with steam-driven machinery.

O L O G Y

1825 The Menier chocolate factory opens at Noisiel in France. In the Netherlands, Van Houten invents his technique for extracting cocoa butter.

1826 Suchard opens a chocolate factory at Serrières in Switzerland. Brillat-Savarin praises the merits of chocolate in his *Physiology of Taste*.

1828 Van Houten invents the first cocoa press and patents the first chocolate powder.

1830 Advances are made in techniques of molding. At his chocolate factory in Lausanne, Switzerland, Charles-Amédée Kohler mixes hazelnuts with chocolate for the first time.

1831 In England, the firm of Cadbury (founded in 1824) starts manufacturing chocolate.

1842 In France, the Barry chocolate factory opens at Meulan.

1847 The Poulain chocolate factory is established at Blois, France. In England, the first chocolate bar makes its appearance.

1861 The Italian chocolate-maker Caffarel creates the *gianduja*, named for Gian d'la Duja, a famous Italian revolutionary.

1870 In Belgium, Jean Neuhaus sets up his company, later to become Côte d'Or.

1875 The Swiss Daniel Peter invents milk chocolate.

1879 Rudolphe Lindt perfects the recipes for coating chocolate and fondant chocolate.

1884 Poulain includes a free metal figurine and colored print in each tin of his chocolate powder.

1894 Milton Hershey founds the Hershey Chocolate Company.

1911 The Callebaut factory opens in Belgium.

1912 The Belgian chocolate-maker Neuhaus invents the praline chocolate.

1914 Banania chocolate-flavored flour is launched in France.

1920 The American Frank Mars creates the Mars Bar.

1950 The Valrhona company is founded in France.

1991 The Chocolate Society is founded in Britain. The Chocolate Club follows in 1994.

1995 Sylvie Douce inaugurates the *Salon du chocolat*, held each October in Paris. A fashion show on the theme of chocolate is among the attractions.

2000 The quality of chocolate in Europe is threatened: under pressure from major manufacturers, some countries demand the right to replace 5 percent cocoa butter with vegetable fats. Master *chocolatiers* oppose the move.

S E L E C T E D · B I B L I O G R A P H Y

Baggett, Nancy. *The International Chocolate Cookbook*. New York: Stewart, Tabori & Chang, 1991.

Bernachon, M. *A Passion for Chocolate*. New York: William Morrow, 1989.

Blanc, Raymond. *Blanc Mange*. London: BBC Books, 1994.

Bourin, Jeanne. *The Book of Chocolate*. Paris: Flammarion, 1996.

Brillat-Savarin, Anthelme. *The Physiology of Taste, or, Meditations on Transcendental Gastronomy*. Washington, D.C.: Counterpoint Press, 1999.

Clarence-Smith, William. *Cocoa and Chocolate, 1765-1914*. London: Routledge, 2000.

Coady, Chantal. *The Chocolate Companion*.

New York: Simon and Schuster, 1995.

Dorchy, Henry and Dorchy, Laure. *The Chocolate Mould : From the Everyday Tool to an Item of Beauty*. Brussels: Éphéméra, 1999.

Greenberg, Hal. *Inside Chocolate: The Chocolate Lover's Guide to Boxed Chocolates*. New York: Harry N. Abrams, 1985.

Linxe, Robert. *La Maison du Chocolat : Transcendent Desserts by the Legendary Chocolatier*. New York: Rizzoli, 2000.

Terrio, Susan. *Crafting the Culture and History of French Chocolate*. Berkeley: University of California Press: 2000.

Young, Allen. *The Chocolate Tree: A Natural History of Cacao*. Washington D.C.: Smithsonian Press, 1994.

INDEX

I N D E X

Photographic credits: Katherine Khodorowski Archives 20, 52, 56, 65 top, 76, 85, 87 bottom, 88 bottom, 100; Kraft-Jacob-Suchard Archives 15, 107; Lindt und Sprüngli Archives 14, 84; Cedus 71; Cioccolata and Cie/G. Brusafferi 44; Kobal Collection 27, 83; R. Opie 74-5; Luisa Ricciarini 12, 60; Marbus Senn 110 top; BARCELONA, Museu de Céramica/R. Ricci 62; BOURNEVILLE, Cadbury Ltd 46–7; DRESDEN, Gemäldegalerie 82; FLORENCE, Biblioteca Nazionale Centrale 103; Scala 86; COLOGNE, Imhoff Stollwerk Museum 68; LONDON, The Bettman Archives 38–9, 96–7, 79; Hulton Deutsch Collection 6, 57, 65 bottom; MADRID, Museo del Prado 78 top; MEULAN, Barry Callebaut cover, 21, 25, 53, 56, 85, 94, 115; MUNICH, Alte Pinakothek 13; NANTERRE, Guillaume de Laubier 18, 42–3, 58; NOISEL, Menier Archives/R. Jeandelle 4–5, 87 top, 88 top, 29 bottom; PARIS, Artephot 34 top, 59, 67, 114; Bibliothèque nationale de France 51, 78, 113; Jean-Pierre Dieterlen 10, 81, 106; Flammarion/F. Morellec 34 bottom, 35, 45 50, 89, 98, 29 top, 109; Hoaqui/E. Valentin 17 /C. Pavard 61; J. Laiter 32–3, 36, 48–9, 54–5, 72–3, 95, 99, 101, 111; musée de l'Homme/D. Destable 11; G. Planchenoult 112; Réunion des musées nationaux 31, 37, 93; Roger-Viollet 42; Scope/J. Gaillard 102; SIP/H. del Olmo 19, 66 /B. Touillon 24; TOP/P. Hussenot 22–3, 105 /Rymen et Cabannes 28, 63, 70; VANVES, Explorer/P. Defoy 41; VEVEY, historical archives Nestlé 80.

Translated and adapted from the French by Barbara Mellor
Additional research by Fui Lee Luk
Color separation: Pollina S.A., France

Originally published as *l'ABCdaire du Chocolat* © 1997 Flammarion
This edition © 2001 Flammarion Inc.

All rights reserved. No part of this publication may be reproduced in any form or by any means without written permission from the publishers.

07 08 09 10 5 4 3 2

ISBN: 987-2-0803-0482-7
Dépôt légal: 04/2001
Printed and bound by Pollina S.A., France - N° L43867

Pages 4–5: W̶ ̶ ̶ ̶ ̶ ̶ ̶ ̶ ̶ ̶ Men